KEYS TO THE APOSTOLIC AND PROPHETIC
Embracing the Authentic
Avoiding the Bizarre

Endorsements

Finally, a sane Biblical examination of the role of the apostolic and prophetic written by Pentecostal authors. This book is a gift to the charismatic and Spirit-filled community, as well as providing others keen insight into the contemporary functioning of these vital elements of ministry.

Dr. George O. Wood
Chairman, World AG Fellowship

Few things are less understood in the western church than apostolic and prophetic functioning. That is why *Keys to the Apostolic and Prophetic* is such an insightful and practical guide. My friends, Dr. Carolyn Tennant and Dr. Joe Girdler, have charted a path forward for the recovery of the full work of God's Spirit in his church today. This book both inspires and instructs, while avoiding the many excesses and pitfalls that have complicated these issues for so many. I highly recommend it!

Dr. James Bradford,
Lead Pastor,
Central Assembly of God, Springfield, MO

The need is great for solid, biblical clarity on the important issue of the apostolic and prophetic in our day in both academia and the ministry field. I'm thankful for the scholarly and practical approach taken by these two very capable authors – Assemblies of God scholars – to give Pentecostal leaders the biblical guidance and tools of wisdom for a healthy path forward.

Donna Barrett, General Secretary,
Assemblies of God USA

I deeply appreciate Dr. Girdler and Dr. Tennant putting in the work necessary to provide solid information to help us all better understand an often avoided and sometimes misappropriated biblical truth. When the God-ordained offices and functions of the Church work according to the grace and authority of Christ, the Church really does equip the saints for the work of the ministry. When the Church does not make room for them to function, the Church suffers and the lost pay for it. Read this with an open heart and an ear to the Spirit. You will be glad you did!

Rick DuBose
General Treasurer of the Assemblies of God USA

Dr. Carolyn Tennant has been a leading voice in the Pentecostal movement for several decades. Together with co-author Dr. Joe Girdler, their experience & depth as theologians and practitioners make this book on the apostolic & prophetic gifts a must read. For those hungry for the Holy Spirit, this book will have a profound impact and provide a Scriptural basis for understanding these powerful gifts given to the Church.

Mark Dean
District Superintendent, Minnesota Assemblies of God

Language matters! Finally, two of the most tainted and falsely represented Kingdom precepts are set back in place by Dr. Carolyn Tennant and Dr. Joseph Girdler. Instead of throwing up their hands and walking away from the apostolic and prophetic because of denominational complications and disunity, their wonderful new book, *Keys to the Apostolic and Prophetic*, provides a welcomed "re-entry" for anyone who feels passive, confused, or even disillusioned about the apostolic and the prophetic. Spread the word; this is a must read for everyone who cares deeply about the health and emergence of God's Kingdom here on earth. This is "Scholarship and Fire" at its very best.

Scott Hagan, Ph.D. Candidate
President, North Central University, Minneapolis

The prospects of the church functioning in a full expression of the ministry gifts of Ephesians 4 provides exciting possibilities. *Keys to the Apostolic and Prophetic: Embracing the Authentic—Avoiding the Bizarre* is the heart-cry of pastors desiring to engage the ministry gifts in a scripturally robust expression, while keeping clear of excesses, misunderstandings, and false claims. I applaud Dr. Tennant and Dr. Girdler for their sane explanation and application of the apostolic and prophetic gifts.

Donald J. Immel
PennDel Ministry Network Superintendent

This book is a long overdue resource to the Body of Christ and, more specifically, to the Pentecostal/Charismatic community. Our failure to properly define the apostolic and prophetic has weakened the Church by neglecting the primacy of these all-important offices. This resource provides clarity and balance on a thoroughly Scriptural and Spirit-empowered platform.

Mark Merrill, D.Min.
District Superintendent, Georgia Assemblies of God

At a time when the Church desperately needs to be Spirit-equipped to address a tsunami of evil and fulfill God's mission, two of the five spiritual gifts given to the Church for mission are frequently misunderstood or avoided altogether. In *Keys to the Apostolic and Prophetic,* Girdler and Tennant set out to provide a contextually balanced and scripturally sound five-fold interpretation of the apostolic and prophetic functions. And they succeed. Both authors are highly qualified to take on this task in terms of biblical academic studies integrated with years of Pentecostal practice and leadership. Girdler and Tennant's work together is a welcome timely contribution toward a stronger Spirit-engaged Church.

Dr. Beth Grant
Executive Presbyter of the Assemblies of God;
Intercultural Educator

As rare scholar-practitioners who illustrate in quotidian life the apostolic and the prophetic, Drs. Girdler and Tennant provide a full and richly textured master class in these vital elements of Spirit-led Christianity for today's church.

Joseph Castleberry, Ed.D.,
President, Northwest University

Finally! A timely, practical tool to grasp these vital but often misunderstood gifts for today's church. Pastors and church leaders who've felt challenged to field questions or teach on this subject will be grateful for the careful, thoughtful way the topic is covered by Dr. Tennant and Dr. Girdler. Ultimately, our churches will be positioned for far greater effectiveness as these neglected gifts are maximized for Kingdom purposes!

John Wootton
Superintendent, Ohio Network Resource Center

Orthodoxy and orthopraxy meet as the authors approach the muddied role and scope of the apostolic and prophetic functions in the church today. The authors' knowledge of Scripture and extensive ministry experience translates into a clear and concise yet profound and relevant book. It is enriching for anyone called to these functions or striving to deepen their understanding of Scripture as it relates to the life of the church. I found it hard to stop reading. I strongly recommend this book.

Armin Colón
International Ministries Pastor,
Oak Creek Assembly of God, WI

Keys to the Apostolic and Prophetic: Embracing the Authentic/ Avoiding the Bizarre is a timely work. Both authors are thoroughly versed in the subject and understand that the apostolic both in office and function is still a part of the church today. You'll want to add this to your theological arsenal.

Ken Draughon,
Alabama District Superintendent, Assemblies of God

The Church needs divinely appointed leaders who embrace spiritual gifts and Spirit-empowered ministry. How tragic to see the role of the Spirit resisted due to instances of "spiritual malpractice." Dr. Tennant and Dr. Girdler provide sound theological and practical perspective to guide the Spirit-led leader.

Kermit S. Bridges, D.Min.
President,
Southwestern Assemblies of God University

Keys to the Apostolic and Prophetic: Embracing the Authentic— Avoiding the Bizarre is perfectly titled, as the authors bring clarity, balance and depth to a topic of great interest, but one laced with confusion. Both Girdler and Tennant write from an educated, yet practical point of view saying both the office and function of Apostle and Prophet are alive and well and need to be recognized. Reading this book is like taking a course, and anyone in ministry will find it very helpful.

Dr. Donald E. Ross
Superintendent, Northwest Ministry Network
and Author of *Turnaround Pastor* and *Tale of Two Churches*

In an era where pushing back darkness and taking new territory should be at the heart of our efforts as disciples of Jesus, we sometimes forget (or have been confused by) some of the crucial gifts He bestowed on the Church to make that possible. Thankfully, in *Keys to the Apostolic and Prophetic: Embracing the Authentic—Avoiding the Bizarre,* authors Girdler and Tennant offer a compelling invitation to explore, embrace, and make use of these priceless giftings, minus the weirdness that puts off and devalues the authentic supernatural work of God through humble, ordinary, but Spirit-empowered lives.

Dr. Jodi Detrick
Author of *The Jesus-Hearted Woman: 10 Leadership Qualities for Enduring & Endearing Influence*, Kirkland, WA

Currently, there is much confusion about how the Biblical offices of Apostle and Prophet apply to contemporary Pentecostal ministry and leadership. Dr Joseph Girdler and Dr Carolyn Tennant effectively expose Scriptural truth and teaching on these important, but often misunderstood, ministries. Further, they offer proper identification and instruction as to how these anointings should properly function in the flow of Spirit led work and worship. Then, with wonderful insight and perfect practicality, they explain how the harmful misuses of these titles can be properly identified and managed. This book is helpful; a great tool for any serious student of these two ministry giftings.

Terry Raburn
Superintendent, Peninsular Florida District Council of the Assemblies of God and Chair of the Board of Trustees, Southeastern University.

Drs. Girdler and Tennant leverage decades of thoughtful academic research and hands-on ministry experience to elevate the discourse on the authentic exercise of apostolic and prophetic ministry. The proliferation of self-proclaimed apostles and prophets, and the disillusionment of those left in their wake, make this clear articulation of true apostolicity and prophetic anointing a must-read for all who long for a genuine outpouring of the Holy Spirit in their local context.

Michael J. Beals, Ph.D.
President, Vanguard University

KEYS TO THE APOSTOLIC AND PROPHETIC
Embracing the Authentic
Avoiding the Bizarre

Joseph S. Girdler
and
Carolyn Tennant

KEYS TO THE APOSTOLIC AND PROPHETIC
© 2019 by Joseph S. Girdler and Carolyn Tennant

All rights reserved. No portion of this book may be reproduced, stored in a retrieval system, or transmitted in any form or by any means, electronic or mechanical, including photocopying, recording, or by an information storage and retrieval system - except by a reviewer who may quote brief passages in a review to be printed in a magazine or newspaper - without permission in writing from the publisher.

Published in Crestwood, Kentucky by **Meadow Stream Publishing.**

All Scripture quotations, unless otherwise indicated, are taken from the Holy Bible, New International Version®, NIV®. Copyright ©1973, 1978, 1984, 2011 by Biblica, Inc.™ Used by permission of Zondervan. All rights reserved worldwide. www. zondervan.com The "NIV" and "New International Version" are trademarks registered in the United States Patent and Trademark Office by Biblica, Inc.™

Scripture quotations taken from the New American Standard Bible® (NASB), Copyright © 1960, 1962, 1963, 1968, 1971, 1972, 1973, 1975, 1977, 1995 by The Lockman Foundation Used by permission. www.Lockman.org

Scripture quotations from The Authorized (King James) Version. Rights in the Authorized Version in the United Kingdom are vested in the Crown. Reproduced by permission of the Crown's patentee, Cambridge University Press.

ISBN 978-1-7337952-4-1 paperback
ISBN 978-1-7337952-5-8 eBook

Dedication

The authors both have deep appreciation developed throughout the years for our friend Dr. Jim Bradford.

His humble kindness, wisdom, strong leadership, and authentic Christianity have greatly impacted and encouraged our lives and ministries. We dedicate this work to him with our profound gratitude for his faithful service to the Kingdom of God.

Table of Contents

Foreword xv
Introduction xix

Chapter One: The Springboard for the Apostolic and Prophetic 1
Chapter Two: The Basic Work of Apostolicity: Pushing Back the
      Darkness 19
Chapter Three: Work Details for Apostolicity 35
Chapter Four: Apostolicity and Relationships 51
Chapter Five: The Prophetic Core 69
Chapter Six: God Uses Creative Prophetic Roles 87
Chapter Seven: Prophetic Worship and Poetic Communication 101
Chapter Eight: The 5 W's and H 115
Chapter Nine: The H: How 129
Chapter Ten: False Prophets and False Apostles 139
Chapter Eleven: Building Discernment 153
Chapter Twelve: Contemporary Problems: Now What? 171

Endnotes 191
About the Authors 197

Foreword

The United States as well as the global population is becoming increasingly biblically illiterate.[1] The problem persists not only in the general population but within the Church as well. Avenues to learning Scripture have been in declination for decades. With no surprise, as biblical literacy decreases, so does understanding the authority of the Kingdom of God and how the Church is meant to function. This results in an impotent institution relying on man's ingenuity and programing.

Regrettably, the role of pastor has been viewed as the catch-all minister who should perform all the functions of leadership in the local church. The pastor is expected to fill the role of teacher who exegetes and expounds Scripture; of the pastor (caretaker) who is available at every family crisis, for counseling, and for hospital visits; of the evangelist who shares the gospel with the community as well as the prophet who proclaims a prophetic utterance in the church or is the one to interpret a tongue. Let's not overlook the role of running the church board and property caretaker! These are just a few of the unrealistic assumptions placed on the role of pastors today. With such an unbiblical job description encompassing every major leadership function, can there be any wonder as to why large numbers of clergy are stepping away from the ministry in despair, defeat, and despondency?

The confusion relating to the role of the modern pastor is largely due to the fact that many Christians are increasingly unsure of what the Bible says regarding church ministry. As a result of their biblical illiteracy, unfeasible expectations are placed upon the pastor's position, and simultaneously the prophetic and apostolic functions are being minimalized.

Amongst most ministry circles there is a reticence coupled with fear to say the words "apostle," "apostolic," and/or "apostolicity." I believe a reason for this hesitancy is an ignorance of what apostolic function is and how it operates as a gift of Jesus to His church. Abuses of the term and title of apostle as well as unbecoming behaviors of soi-disant apostles have led many in the church to assume an obdurate posture towards the legitimacy of any apostolicity operating today.

Drs. Tennant and Girdler biblically and courageously address the gift of the apostle in the Early Church and the apostolic function operating through many individuals and organizations today. In *Keys to the Apostolic and Prophetic,* they clearly and pragmatically define the apostolic function, showing how it results in the personal health of ministers and the local body of believers.

God still speaks to His Church today. One way in which He communicates is through the prophetic word, and as the authors expound, God intends prophecy to be in full operation. Their book explicates how prophecy appropriately operates in the church and in the marketplace.

In May 2016, a prophetic word began to come forward through multiple, credible sources that we were about to witness the greatest student awakening in history.[2] An important and interesting part of this prophetic word is that this would be an awakening of Kingdom power and covering. I am convinced that this will be a worldwide awakening which will cross ministry and denominational boundaries.

How do we know this is a true prophetic word? It was brought before the elders—those in campus ministry who walk in apostolicity affirmed the veracity of the prophetic word. As the apostolic elders and leaders of campus ministry stepped out in faith and belief that this word was from God, the nascent stages of awakening are being observed, further affirming the prophetic word as veritable. If a prophetic word is true, it will come to pass.

Further, we are observing a hunger for God and a move of His Holy Spirit in a greater level amongst university students and campus ministry leaders than we have experienced in decades. God is moving in ways we have not seen, possibly ever.

What will maintain this awakening and move of God? One critical factor will be what the Lord said in the prophetic word: it will be an awakening of Kingdom covering. Where does this Kingdom covering come from? It comes from those walking in apostolicity and the prophetic. This is why this book is so critical to the Church today. We must come to a clear understanding of apostolic and prophetic functions in order to fulfill God's purposes as we approach the coming of the age. The Church must acknowledge, value, and operate in apostolicity and the prophetic for this is where spiritual awakening hinges and will be propelled.

Drs. Tennant and Girdler are far more than academicians; they are practitioners. They write out of personal experience and Kingdom revelation. *Keys to the Apostolic and Prophetic* is a gift to the church that I believe is prophetic itself. As the national senior director of a large nationwide and worldwide ministry, it is my desire that all our missionaries, staff, and students would hunger to minister apostolically and prophetically but would always discern and acknowledge that these authentic ministries originate only from God. I wish this for the entire global Church.

I am an ardent supporter of the message communicated in *Keys to the Apostolic and Prophetic*, and I am convinced as the Church embraces the Kingdom premise of the book, we will advance the Kingdom of God in ways not yet seen.

E. Scott Martin
National Senior Director
Chi Alpha Campus Ministries, U.S.A

Introduction

Addressing a Contemporary Dilemma

When asked who he was, prophet John the Baptist used Isaiah's words saying, "I am the voice of one crying in the wilderness, 'Make straight the path for the Lord'" (John 1:23). The work of prophecy points to and prepares the way for God to enter in amongst mankind. Likewise, the apostolic function of strengthening and expanding the church is deeply needed before Jesus returns.

Now is the time to refresh and actuate both the apostolic and prophetic. So much calls for Christian voice and action: Increased population with millions who do not know Christ; escalating crime, strife, immorality, and injustice; unbridled egotism, spiteful opinionation, and lack of love; growing fear and godlessness; shrinking church attendance and flagging commitment to spiritual things. Such are our challenges.

The Lord has much to tell us about how the Church can advance in these shifting times, but we need to get better at listening. Church leaders should be posturing less and paying more attention to what the Spirit is saying. Exactly how can we make inroads and establish the church in dark places? How do we hear God's directions, guidance, and encouragement? This book is designed to offer some of the keys.

Both apostolic and prophetic functions have waned at the very moment they are desperately needed. Today, as in Samuel's day, "[t]he word of the Lord was rare; there were not many visions" (1 Sam. 3:1). Fully-faceted prophetic work is generally infrequent and unnoticed. Likewise, when it comes to the Church's apostolic expansion, increase in Christianity is not even keeping pace with population growth.[3] Satan is holding a vice-like grip in multiple strongholds around the world.

Though both God-empowered apostolic and prophetic functions are crucial to the Church's development and health, false prophets and apostles are escalating by the droves. The Apostle

Paul warned of deceptive apostles and counterfeit workers cloaking themselves as apostles of Christ (2 Cor. 11:13). Today's Church and her leadership indicate rising concerns regarding those who proclaim themselves as experts, desire power and attention, and assert themselves as carrying the title of an apostle or prophet. The impersonators are deceiving and confusing the flock, asserting unhealthy dominance. Some are losing sight of their true purposes as they chase fads and destructive theological pursuits without scriptural foundations. These distractions frequently bring both doctrinal disturbances and grave consequences to the body of Christ when not addressed properly.

What are the keys to dealing with such problems? If someone comes into the church and starts delivering false prophecies, what then? When church members are drawn away to conferences by a "super-apostle," what should be the response? How do we handle the bizarre occurrences that may surface in the apostolic and prophetic? Can we recognize and encourage the authentic? Sometimes, a person or word will seem a little off, or we are checked in our spirit, but is that enough to stop it? How can we do a better job of discerning what is on target and what is not? This book is not merely in opposition to certain things—it actually advocates for the real work of God, so both will be studied carefully.

Numerous concerns with false apostles and prophets presently challenge today's Church. In response, the temptation is to limit or stop apostolic and prophetic work altogether. If these can be avoided, it is reasoned, that should handle the difficulties. However, quenching the work of the Spirit at such a critical crossroads from modernity to postmodernity is definitely not the answer. Now is the time for the Church to move forward according to God's direction and Spirit-power, and much of this emerges through apostolic and prophetic functioning.

The topics of apostle and prophet tend to promote wariness, and as a result, many Pentecostals in particular are reticent to broach the topic or teach on it. Indeed, it can be baffling to choose the right keys to unlock the truth. Perhaps we, the authors, are presumptuous to even give this a try. The areas are messy, and it is very tempting to leave them alone. Still, we have been asked by so many people to write this book and prompted by the Spirit to share our studies, so we have tackled it and humbly hand to you our attempts at releasing the padlock to these two mysterious functions. There are some in Charismatic circles or among those proclaiming themselves as prophets or apostles who are writing on these topics for today's church, but there are few, if any, trusted voices in the Pentecostal milieu who are offering aid. We hope this helps.

The prophetic and apostolic functions are not mysterious to God, but history has muddied the waters and brought lack of clarity regarding what this work is actually meant to entail. As the chapters of the book unfold, it should become increasingly clear that God intended these ministries to function in a broad capacity throughout the everyday life of the Church. They are naturally carried out by God's servants through the supernatural working of the Spirit. The apostolic and prophetic are God-given roles designed to strengthen, train, and help bring the Church to maturity and wholeness.

The apostolic and prophetic should not overpower other roles but rather provide complementary support.

While the spiritual roles of pastors, teachers, and evangelists have readily been accepted by mainstream Christian cultures, the seasoned mantles of those who function in prophetic and apostolic gifts are likewise essential for a balanced maturity as co-heirs and partakers in the Kingdom of God (e.g., Eph. 4:11; 1 Cor. 12-14).

The book makes some assumptions. The authors both feel that in this day of rising false apostles and prophets, it is best not to use titles except when referring to Old and New Testament apostles and prophets. We will flesh out our reasoning as we go along. That being said, we cannot be more committed to releasing a full flow of the apostolic and prophetic functioning in our day and age. This can be realized as church people become involved in the flow of the Spirit.

Never has God's plan been to develop a group of "super-apostles" or "super-prophets" who set themselves above others beyond the church context. Rather He uses many as both leaders and workers to function as a broad base in apostolic and prophetic work. These two ministries were not designed to overpower the roles of pastors, evangelists, and teachers but rather to provide complementary support and action. Neither the prophetic nor apostolic should ever seek to be the most important and influential roles in the church. Instead they should see themselves as servants whose gifts are among a group of gifts that are all essential and dependent upon the others to complete the body of Christ.

What does apostolic and prophetic work even look like? So many people have asked this, that the book was designed to go in-depth regarding prophecy and apostolicity, demonstrating the wide variety of operation that God intends. This material is supported by a wide range of Scripture we felt essential to include. Both of us have done extensive biblical research on these topics. Our commitment to Bible-based doctrine and understanding requires that we share multiple Scripture passages on these topics rather than simply give our unsupported opinions. This should help the reader understand our conclusions, assist in personal study, aid in spiritual discernment, and provide the background needed to train others in turn. The book is designed to help an individual function in wiser and better ways if called to either apostolic or prophetic ministries. Additionally, these chapters should help everyone understand, support, and encourage those individuals specifically called to these functions.

Joel 2:28 says,

> And afterward, I will pour out my Spirit on all people. Your sons and daughters will prophesy, your old men will dream dreams, your young men will see visions.

Our Pentecostal roots started with this sort of outpouring (Acts 2) and call for its continuation and our involvement. If lack of understanding and confusion regarding the apostolic and prophetic causes us to quench the authentic pouring out of God's Spirit, this would be most sad indeed. We are a people of the Spirit who say we desire to have Him flow in our midst, and He yearns to do just that in even greater ways.

Who are the authors? While both have contributed to this overall work, Joseph Girdler, D.Min, wrote his doctoral dissertation[4] for the Assemblies of God Theological Seminary (AGTS) at Evangel University on the topic of "apostolicity" which refers to the context of someone today who properly functions with apostolic purposes. He further considered how this calling goes hand in hand with the callings of denominational and network leaders. The ideas presented here on this topic are primarily developed from his project research and are coupled with over three decades of pastoral and denominational leadership. In his present role as Superintendent of the Kentucky Assemblies of God, he brings considerable personal and practical experience to the subject matter, uniquely contributing to this work.

Carolyn Tennant, Ph.D., has lectured about and ministered in the prophetic in various settings around the world, including involvement in the Argentine revival. Having served at North Central University (Minneapolis) for three decades as a professor and vice president, she often mentors young people growing in their prophetic calling. Still speaking around the U.S. and teaching in the D.Min program at AGTS, Carolyn has seen the confusion many have about this vital area of the church, leading to the writing of her recent book on the five-fold ministry.[5]

In the first chapter of this book we will consider God's selection process for apostolic and prophetic roles. In the next eight chapters we will take the advice of those who teach on the topics of counterfeiting and forgery. These experts have their students focus on the details of authentic money, documents, and art, because in learning those, they will be far more capable of spotting the fakes and frauds. Therefore, readers will find some chapters on the apostolic followed by some on the prophetic, where we will see what can be learned from Scripture about the proper functioning of these roles. After this, the final three chapters will apply our findings to the Church today. Also considered will be the problems entangled when there is divergence from the proper functioning of apostolicity and the prophetic. Skills in discernment will be honed. Let's begin our revealing journey and turn some new keys.

Chapter One

The Springboard for the Apostolic and Prophetic

"So Christ Himself gave the apostles, the prophets..."
Ephesians 4:11

The concepts of both the apostolic and prophetic are foggy to the majority of church attenders. This lack of clarity often begins with church leaders who hardly know what to teach or say about it. Problems in these two ministry functions abound and cause wariness. Many seem reticent to fully embrace the prophetic and apostolic areas and often avoid these scriptural doctrines altogether.

Present Wariness and Lack of Understanding
We have come to the place where we've commissioned generations of pastors who have never personally experienced true revival. Many leaders have not seen for themselves a flow of genuine prophetic ministry. Some were not raised in a Pentecostal atmosphere and missed training on how to pastor the apostolic and prophetic gifts.

At times they found what some tout as the "gifts" to be confusing and divisive to a church body. Encountering some of these spurious forms, congregants can sit there, tilting their heads to the side in wonder, and ultimately withholding their tithes, involvement, and trust – even to the point of leaving the church. They settle for "the safe church down the street" where neither they nor their children will be scared or burned, pushed over, or made to feel guilty if they don't follow the human manipulation. A number of pastors today avoid Pentecostal ministry, not because they don't read it in scripture or are closed to the Spirit, but because they have personally experienced the false and want no part of it.

A scripturally sound five-fold interpretation is imperative for the Church.

Both of the authors have also met numerous pastors and parishioners from non-Pentecostal or non-Charismatic fellowships who personally have had a Pentecostal experience but choose to keep it private. What is therefore increasingly occurring across America is that churches and leaders have simply opted not to allow the gifts to be used at all during a public service. Such a stifling is happening simultaneously with a rise in prophetic and apostolic ministries across the globe. In the midst of all this, a contextually balanced and scripturally sound five-fold interpretation is imperative for the church to accomplish what God has designed for His people.

Apostles and Prophets: A Little History

What are some of our scriptural keys to a fundamental understanding of the apostolic and prophetic? In Hebrews 3:1, Jesus Himself is called our apostle and high priest. Indeed, Jesus was *sent by God for a particular mission*—the basic meaning of "apostle." With Him was a group of disciples who carried the mantle of "apostle," saw Jesus with their own eyes, and witnessed His resurrection (Acts 1:21-22). They were sent with authority as messengers to establish the Church and develop new Kingdom initiatives, while simultaneously guarding doctrine, maintaining purity through disciplinary measures, and providing a network of Christian workers. The term "apostles of Christ" was used interchangeably for the twelve disciples of Jesus (Matt. 10:2, Mark 3:14 and 6:30, Luke 9:10 and 17:1, 5 and 22:14 and 24:10) and included Matthias who, after prayer, was called out as an apostle to replace Judas (Acts 1:21-26). Many place Paul among these "apostles of Christ" since he had a vision of Jesus in his striking conversion and thereafter consistently lived out his apostolic calling and used the title (1 Cor. 1:1; cf. 2 Cor. 1:1; Gal. 1:1; Eph. 1:1; Col. 1:1; et al.)

Others beyond the twelve were named as "apostles of the

church." Scripture mentions the following: Barnabas and Paul (Acts 14:3-4, 14 and 1 Cor. 9:1-6 and Rom. 1:1); both Silas and Paul (1 Thess. 2:6 and 1:1-6); Apollos (1 Cor. 4:6-9); Epaphroditus (Phil. 2:25); Andronicus and Junia(s) (probably a woman) (Rom. 16:7). These apostles were sent out with missionary roles and humbly served the Church.

Ephesians 4:11-13 mentions both the apostle and prophet as two of five gifts that Jesus gave to the Church after His victory over Satan and His consequent resurrection:

So Christ himself gave the apostles, the prophets, the evangelists, the pastors and teachers, to equip his people for works of service, so that the body of Christ may be built up, until we all reach unity in the faith and in the knowledge of the Son of God and become mature, attaining to the whole measure of the fullness of Christ.

Many believe the offices of the apostle and prophet ended around 96 A.D. when the last living disciple, John, died. Vinson Synan, enumerating the history of apostles, writes, "Over time, as the bishops consolidated their power in the church, the office of apostle was almost forgotten. In fact, by the second century, apostles and prophets were seen as little more than traveling medicine men with little or no influence or authority."[6] He goes on to explain that the apostolic and prophetic roles both became less and less clear. Even the role of evangelist lost its conceptual clarity until Charles Finney renewed the perception of that role in the 19th century. This left only the two roles of pastor and teacher.

For centuries the Church put primary emphasis upon pastor/ teacher, stifling the other three gifts.

For multiple centuries, the Church functioned with primary emphasis upon pastor and teacher to the extent of stifling the other three gifts Christ designed for the Church's effectual operation. When teaching was extremely diluted or missing historically, a one-fold ministry resulted. This has significantly weakened the advance and health of the Church throughout the ages. Considering the importance of authentic evangelistic, prophetic, and apostolic functions in advancing God's work, Satan has tried hard to halt their beneficial and strengthening effects in the Church.

Thankfully there were a few glimmers of powerful apostolic work throughout the years or we might not even be here to speak of this. God raised up strong apostolic leaders such as Patrick in Ireland along with succeeding converts like Columba, Columbanus, and others who during the 5th-7th centuries spread out across Scotland and continental Europe, bravely reaching out to the "barbaric" tribes. Then there was Count von Zinzendorf in the 18th century who coupled a new wave of evangelism and church planting with continual prayer, reaching numerous countries with Moravian missionaries and inspiring William Carey, the first English missionary. But even amidst these and a few other shining examples of apostolicity, there are decades and centuries when the Word was not adequately spread and apostolic advancement languished. Think what the world might be like now if apostolicity had remained strong as God intended.

The lack of proper functioning in the apostolic and prophetic ministries for centuries led to a proliferation of problems. The general absence of clear roles coupled with few God-ordained models has left room for false prophets and false apostles to thrive. Today there is little instruction on what the real functions should look like. Therefore, the Church does not readily recognize those truly called into the prophetic or apostolic functions, nor does she always identify the fraudulent. When the Church manages to uncover deception, the realization understandably raises everybody's guard against the prophetic and apostolic—both true and false. Anyone properly called and functioning in these giftings today runs the risk of being added to the false category almost automatically.

The preponderance of false prophets and apostles should not be particularly surprising since Jesus Himself prophesied that false Messiahs and false prophets would appear and even perform great signs and wonders in the end times (Matt. 24:23-15). Many today are usurping the titles and warping the authentic roles as we shall see in later chapters. Therefore, the authors will avoid the terms of "prophet" and "apostle" in today's contexts, and rather than centering upon titles and positions, we will instead focus upon the functioning of these roles. We will utilize words like "prophetic," "apostolic," and "apostolicity" unless we are referring directly to Old Testament and New Testament prophets and apostles.

"Apostolicity" is the context of someone today functioning with apostolic purpose(s). Apostolic function includes the leadership principles and endeavors given to apostolicity.

Working in the prophetic entails declaring, expressing, and predicting God's divine will. Prophetic function is likewise the leadership principles and endeavors given to those who operate in the prophetic on a regular basis.

The proper involvement in both the apostolic and prophetic requires individuals' genuine humility, real servanthood, a call, commissioning from the Lord, and demonstration of the fruit of the Spirit. In their heart, there is no desire for the "limelight" or personal power. They know the need to spend much time in prayer and stay attached to the vine, living in the Spirit.

Proper apostolic and prophetic functioning are relevant and significant for today's postmodern, pluralistic, biblically illiterate, and doctrinally challenged society. God will prepare the ones He calls to these roles both to lead out and to experience one of the greatest outpourings of the Holy Spirit He has ever sent to the earth. Apostolic and prophetic topics need to be moved to the forefront of our thinking in preparation for what God wants to do.

Called Out By God as His Representatives

Leadership in the church is certainly a calling by God, and no one should strive to attain roles of authority, spiritual mantles of assumed respect, or any of the Ephesians 4:11 five-fold responsibilities aside from a clear sense of God's directive.

The original Greek word for apostle was *apostolos*, and it meant one sent for specific purposes or mission(s). Historically, missionaries, ambassadors, delegates, and emissaries were each an example of this word. They were called upon for a particular task and sent out to accomplish it with full authority to represent the one who chose them. With eighty occurrences of the word *apostolos* and its cognates in the New Testament, obviously it was an important concept for the functioning of the early church.

In pre-first-century thought, prior to being a term referring to Christian ministry, the word *apostolos* was closely related to seafaring envoys. The term was not originally developed by the Early Church but rather was adopted from secular uses.

Further, in Palestinian Judaism, the Hebrew word *shaliach*

was the Hebraic equivalent of the Greek word for apostle. The *shaliach* was an ambassador, agent, or emissary. The Jews knew it as a Torah legal term for a person who was empowered by someone else to act on his behalf.

The first use of the word in the Old Testament referred to Eliezer, the servant of Abraham, who was commissioned to find a suitable wife for Abraham's son Isaac from among his own people. Legally, the *shaliach* was authorized to act on behalf of the sender. It was as if Eliezer were Abraham, having power to do whatever Abraham could do. As such, the *shaliach* did not give up his own personality, style, intellect, resourcefulness, creativity, and choice. He used them freely on behalf of the one he represented.

Another example is Moses. Exodus 7:1 tells us, "Now the Lord said to Moses, 'See, I have made you like God to Pharaoh, and your brother Aaron will be your prophet.'" This is not at all to be misunderstood as saying that Moses was God, but rather he would be a representative of God's. We then see Moses performing miracles and signs through God's power, just like the New Testament apostles.

The ancient prophets were also considered to be *shaliachs*, sent ones. Elisha and Elijah received the power and authority to raise the dead. Elisha miraculously made a little food to be stretched so it fed many, and Elijah caused a widow's food not to run out. Prophets were commissioned to deliver a message, and God had certain purposes He wanted to accomplish. God clearly "sent" Isaiah (Isa. 6:8), Jeremiah (Je. 1:7), Ezekiel (Ez. 3:5), and Malachi (Mal. 4:5). These were given authority to speak and were backed up by miracles, signs, and wonders.

To the Jewish mind, the *shaliach* was the agent or representative, and therefore he was to be treated just as if he were the person who sent him. Anything Moses or the other prophets did would be regarded as if it were God Himself. This explains on an even deeper level why it was very important for Moses not to strike the rock when God told him to speak to it instead (Num. 20:2-13). God was so directly associated with Moses in the Hebrews' perspective that when Moses showed unrestrained frustration and anger with a strike, this would be representative of God Himself. Anyone this closely identified with God must evidence precise obedience.

Today's leaders need to keep this in mind.

Apostles and prophets were commissioned to their tasks and sent out as the representatives of God.

This historic root of the apostle makes it clear there is one insurmountable requirement. Anyone functioning in the apostolic or prophetic must be called to the role. It is their spiritual duty and obligation to be commissioned to their tasks and always keep in mind they have been sent out as the agents or representatives of God Himself.

No one truly called to the prophetic should ever say anything contrary to what their sender wishes. They are not representing themselves; they are representing God. Likewise, the apostolic functions emerge directly out of the orders from God. They are called for particular assignments in certain places and will be given the power and authority to function in those specific roles. Prophets are not to speak their own words and ideas. Apostles are not to do what they desire and claim personal power and authority for their own tasks. Rather, authority is given only for assigned responsibilities and not for everything an individual may want to do on his own.

The Prophetic Calling

Studying the calling of some of the prophets in Scripture is most enlightening. We can learn a great deal about the role and what God expects to accomplish with the prophetic. Ezekiel 2:1-8 is a good place to begin since it indicates the paradigm for the calling of a prophet:

> He said to me {Ezekiel}, "Son of man, stand up on your feet and I will speak to you!" As He spoke, the Spirit came in to me and raised me to my feet; and I heard Him speaking to me. He said, "Son of man, I am sending you to the Israelites, to a rebellious nation that has rebelled against Me; they and their ancestors have been in revolt against Me to this very day. The people to whom I am sending you are obstinate and stubborn. Say to them, 'This is what the Sovereign Lord says.' And whether they listen or fail to listen—for they are a rebellious people—they will know that a prophet has been among them. And you, son of man, do not be afraid of them nor their words. Do not be afraid though briers and thorns are all around you and you live with scorpions. Do not be afraid of what they say or be terrified by them, though they are a rebellious people. You must speak my words to them, whether they listen or fail to listen, for they are rebellious.

But you, son of man, listen to what I say to you. Do not rebel like that rebellious people; open your mouth and eat what I give you."

Clearly, Ezekiel evidenced a fear of the Lord: he had fallen on his face in the presence of God and was empowered by the Spirit to stand back up on his feet. All those working in the prophetic need to experience the Spirit entering into them (v. 1), empowering the tasks to which they have been called. It is not an easy thing to be sent to those who have rebelled against God, people who are not wanting to hear what God has to say to them. This task is just as challenging today. But those functioning in the prophetic must fear the Lord more than man so they say exactly what the Lord wants them to say, no more and no less. They should never add anything, and they must not subtract anything. They may not change the message nor make it easier or softer. Even though the people who receive the prophecy may be "obstinate and stubborn" (v. 4) and will not listen, the prophetic word still needs to be given "whether they listen or fail to listen" (v. 7).

Ezekiel's call included an exhortation not to fear or be dismayed by these rebellious people even "though briers and thorns are all around you and you live with scorpions" (v. 6). Who wants this job? Anybody who would desire to be called as a prophet is probably naïve, or they have wrong motives, wishing they could have personal power to say what they want, be heard and praised, and even "tell people off." The prophetic calling, however, is not a "fun" job.

Those who are authentically called of the Lord find it hard at times to share what He wants. Though many prophetic words are not difficult to impart, some are. They might bring a warning or a correction that needs to be heeded. However, these words too must be released. If a person tries to hold in a message God wants delivered, that word will burn to get out. God did not intend for it to be retained by the messenger; the dispatch was meant to be shared.

Jeremiah, another prophet who was clearly called, described this challenge of sharing God's word in Jeremiah 20:8-10:

> Whenever I speak, I cry out proclaiming violence and destruction. So the word of the LORD has brought me insult and reproach all day long. But if I say, "I will not mention his word or speak anymore in his name," his word is in my heart like a fire, a fire shut up in my bones. I am weary of holding it in; indeed, I cannot. I hear many whispering "Terror on every side! Denounce him! Let's denounce him!"

Earlier, in the first chapter, he told of God coming to him. The Lord revealed that He knew Jeremiah before he was formed in the womb—that He had set him apart, appointing him as a prophet to the nations. Jeremiah responded humbly. He told the Lord that he didn't know how to speak because he was too young, but God told him not to think this way. "You must go to everyone I send you to and say whatever I command you" (v. 7).

The necessity of obedience is apparent.

The necessity of obedience is apparent. Being called as a prophet is serious and seems almost impossible to carry out, but Jeremiah 1:9 goes on to assure us: "Then the Lord reached out his hand and touched my mouth and said to me, 'I have put my words in your mouth.'" God will purify and prepare His prophetic voices.

This preparation also transpired with Isaiah, and we see the same pattern for God's call. Isaiah 6:5-7 shows an interaction after Isaiah had been given a vision of the glory of the Lord.

"Woe to me!" I [Isaiah] cried. "I am ruined! For I am a man of unclean lips, and I live among a people of unclean lips, and my eyes have seen the King, the LORD Almighty." Then one of the seraphim flew to me with a live coal in his hand, which he had taken with tongs from the altar. With it he touched my mouth and said, "See, this has touched your lips; your guilt is taken away and your sin atoned for."

When there is a genuine prophetic utterance, God's words have been placed in the messenger's mouth, and it is important for those very words to come forth. Humans naturally feel unable to do this, sensing unholiness and the inability to speak on God's behalf. But He calls people to share His words nonetheless. God provides the cleansing needed and enables them to carry out what He intends. His anointing is mandatory because humans cannot do this work by themselves.

God says in Numbers 12:6,

"When there is a prophet among you, I, the LORD, reveal myself to them in visions, I speak to them in dreams."

God reveals not only His words but His very self. When individuals are truly called to the prophetic, they are humble, feeling basically unable and unworthy of doing what God has required of them, yet they are having a revelation of God and His purposes. The message they receive is well rounded, full of God's personality and character. They follow through out of pure obedience and faith that God will be with them in the Spirit as they deliver the words He desires.

When we are authentically called by God to the prophetic, the word of God comes to us; we do not find the word! A word from God cannot be conjured up on demand. He gives a word when and if He wishes. In Joel 1:1, Hosea 1:1, and Ezekiel 1:3, each passage states the word of the Lord "came unto" that prophet.

The prophetic word of God comes to us; we do not find the word.

Samuel 3:1-11 reveals that in "those days the word of the LORD was rare; there were not many visions." Neither Eli nor Samuel even understood the call of the Lord, but call He did! The boy Samuel had not even had the opportunity to learn what the prophetic looked like or how it was received. Yet, God had important and difficult things to say to Eli, and young Samuel was required to tell him and leave nothing out.

One way to examine the heart of a prophetic person is to inquire and learn about their call from God. Did they grasp for their position? Or was there a reluctance, a sense of unworthiness, but nonetheless, a clear summoning from the Lord? People truly called by God are unpretentious. A key element is their willingness to submit to suggestions and counsel. They long to learn and grow in the prophetic, knowing they have been called to the almost formidable and undeniably overwhelming task of speaking what God wants to say. Their desire is to do it right and take correction well. They are unassuming and simply desire to obey God.

The prophet's calling was known to many. The biblical prophets were recognized and acknowledged by their Old Testament Jewish tribe or New Testament local church as being tapped by God for the prophetic function. None were self-appointed or out to make a name for themselves. Popularity was not really a possibility. Their names were not type-set onto posters nor their most recent conferences put up on social media. They did the best they could because they loved God and determined to serve Him, no matter what.

The Apostolic Calling
Answering the call of God is the initial step for an apostolic leader.

In Galatians 1:1 Paul states he was an apostle "sent not from men nor by a man, but by Jesus Christ and God the Father." Like the specific callings of the prophets, the apostles were also set apart by God Himself. According to Galatians 1:15-17, Paul recognized his apostolic commission was from birth and that he had been separated by God's grace for the proclamation of the gospel.

A further review of Acts 13:2-3 offers an encapsulated summary of the divine calling of two apostles: "While they were worshiping the Lord and fasting, the Holy Spirit said, 'Set apart for me Barnabas and Saul for the work to which I have called them,' So after they had fasted and prayed, they placed their hands on them and sent them off."

The Church today and certainly its leaders must be faithful in worship and fasting to hear clearly the direction of the Holy Spirit. Fasting (abstaining from food and certain activities) and replacing "self" with prayer and other spiritual concerns are of utmost importance for effectual spiritual leadership. Fasting is not a "work" that somehow earns deserved grace from God. Rather, the exclusion of outside stimuli, including food, aids the believer in becoming more sensitive to the voice and leading of the Holy Spirit. Acts 13 and other verses indicate that fasting, prayer, and waiting on God were the norm in the Early Church. Today's Church has lost the urgency to pray in this manner. Leonard Ravenhill said, "The greatest undiscovered area in the resources of God is the place of prayer."7 In this case, prayer resulted in the tremendous sourcing of Paul and Barnabas. Think about what the Early Church would have missed without Paul's three missionary journeys!

Apostolicity comes forth from the church community in prayer.

The Acts 13 account, coming out of corporate fasting and prayer (not just individuals doing it separately), indicates a clear community involvement in the calling of apostles. Both Paul and Barnabas were sent and commissioned by the church at Antioch. According to Acts 13:1, this church had strong leaders who knew how to hear from God, including five teachers and prophets. The church fasted, worshiped, and prayed for an unspecified period, taking time to receive God's direction. They recognized and acknowledged the particular call of God through the Holy

Spirit, and then they corporately commissioned Paul and Barnabas, sending them off on their first missionary journey.

These are key elements to the apostolic anointing of the Holy Spirit upon an individual's life and ministry. Apostolicity gushes forth from the realm of the church community as they seek God's will and jointly gain discernment regarding His plan. This is not based upon one individual's personal desire for a role or a title. In short, no people send themselves off for apostolic work. It is the church community that sends them off, provides the spiritual covering, and conveys a further level of accountability for their sending—something missing too often in today's self-proclaimed apostolic voices.

The book of Acts clearly demonstrates Luke's pervasive emphasis on the Holy Spirit's involvement in empowering and anointing for spiritual service. People do not enter apostolicity simply by the election of peers, a colleague who proclaims them as such, or by their own announcement, but rather only by the choice of the Lord Jesus Christ. The church helps to discern and acknowledge what the Holy Spirit is doing within the individual and then supports and affirms that ministry.

To further understand the apostolic calling of Paul and Barnabas, we need to consider the context of the church at Antioch. Gentiles in that city were already being taught by both Paul and Barnabas, and Antioch would soon become the chief center for sending out missionaries with apostolic mantles. Paul's three missionary journeys are described in Acts 13-18, and all of them occurred after Peter had his vision regarding the Gentiles and went to Cornelius (Acts 10), followed by doctrinal discussion in Jerusalem about Gentiles coming into the Church (Acts 11:1-18).

Speaking of Antioch as the apostolic hub, A.T. Robertson makes an interesting point regarding Acts 13: "Luke here begins the second part of Acts with Antioch as the center of operations, no longer Jerusalem. Paul is now the central figure instead of Peter. Jerusalem had hesitated too long to carry out the command of Jesus to take the gospel to the whole world. That glory will now belong to Antioch."[8] Windows of opportunity do not last long. God speaks and the discerning apostolic leader responds.

If a church doesn't take apostolic advancement seriously, God looks to those who will.

We can learn a crucial lesson here. God clearly expects leadership to be concerned about apostolic functions and commissioning. The whole world was to be affected by the death of His Son, not just Israel. The Lord requires His Church to move out and go into uncharted territory to spread the gospel. When a church does not take apostolic advancement seriously, God shifts the emphasis to a place where people are willing to take up the task.

Considering the many places Paul and other apostles to the Gentiles reached, it is sobering to consider what would have happened if the Antioch church had not taken their apostolic "sending mission" seriously. If what is recorded after Acts 13 were to be chopped off, the rooting of the Early Church would have been far different. A lack of the apostolic flow has tremendous ramifications which the church could not afford then, nor can it afford now. We must be seriously mindful of apostolicity if the Church is to complete its task before Jesus returns.

Today's Church, as did Antioch, must be willing to invest time in fasting and prayer as they seek the Lord to discern the most effective ways to carry out thrusts into dark places and effectively reach the lost. This is not the adoption of a program or strategy but rather a pursuit of God's direction and of His provision for anointed, apostolic leadership. This important, corporate prayer step is often skipped in contemporary church circles. Without it, man-made approaches with human-appointed leaders will attempt to do what can only be propelled and led properly by the Holy Spirit. E.M. Bounds penned these words over one hundred years ago, still ringing true today: "What the Church needs today is not more machinery or better, not new organizations or more and novel methods, but men and women... mighty in prayer."[11]

We must return to being a people of prayer, instead of simply holding prayer meetings. In many places, even the prayer meetings are diminished. Antioch became an apostolic center birthed in a praying community of believers. It was their habit and part of their daily living.

We must return to being a people of prayer, instead of simply holding prayer meetings.

After praying and searching for God's plan to reach the Gentiles, the church at Antioch laid hands on Barnabas and Saul and sent them off to do what the Holy Spirit led them to accomplish. The commissioning signified the recognition of God's call on the lives of these men and also indicated that the church identified with them as their representatives for God's work. Paul and Barnabas were sent with two distinct affirmations: that of the Holy Spirit and that of the church. By this, God's divine choice was noted by all, and the people recognized the Spirit's intentional extension of the church into Judea, Samaria, and beyond. This paradigm is still possible and needed today for the apostolic.

Likely throughout this process, many Gentile believers in the church at Antioch, under the Spirit's guidance, purposefully set their hearts to finding a way to send the gospel beyond Antioch and around the world so other Gentiles might come to know Christ, as they had. Apostolicity was on their hearts. It is also imperative to note that the specific persons mentioned in this selection process are prophets and teachers, thus excluding the hierarchical notion that apostles had authority over all other ministers and ministries in the New Testament. If that were the case, only an apostle would be able to commission other apostles.

Checks and Balances

Both prophets and apostles evidenced a system of checks and balances which must be clearly understood. A key to this is an apostolic example found in Galatians 2:1-10. Although a little long, the whole context is essential:

> Then after fourteen years, I went up again to Jerusalem, this time with Barnabas. I took Titus along also. I went in response to a revelation and, meeting privately with those esteemed as leaders, I presented to them the gospel that I preach among the Gentiles. I wanted to be sure I was not running and had not been running my race in vain...
>
> As for those who were held in high esteem—whatever they were makes no difference to me; God does not show favoritism—they added nothing to my message. On the contrary, they recognized that I had been entrusted with the task of preaching the gospel to the uncircumcised, just as Peter had been to the circumcised. For God, who was at work

in Peter as an apostle to the circumcised, was also at work in me as an apostle to the Gentiles. James, Cephas and John, those esteemed as pillars, gave me and Barnabas the right hand of fellowship when they recognized the grace given to me. They agreed that we should go to the Gentiles, and they to the circumcised. All they asked was that we should continue to remember the poor, the very thing I had been eager to do all along. Galatians 2:1–2, 6–10.

Notice Paul voluntarily went to Jerusalem and submitted himself and his apostolic message and ministry to the other leaders. He did not come to argue they too should go to the Gentiles, nor was Paul in any way trying to push his own agenda, approach, or even doctrine. He had received a revelation, and rather than making him haughty, this revelation led him to the conclusion that he needed to talk with others and ask their advice.

Those truly called to the apostolic are respectful, desiring to have a spiritual covering and willing to submit themselves to other leaders whom they know carry the church's authority. They realize it is not sufficient to choose their own accountability group from among friends with whom they personally feel comfortable (as some self-proclaimed apostles are presently doing). The Jerusalem leaders were perceptive, recognizing the grace given to Paul. They did not require him to change anything at all, except to remember the poor, which anyone would likewise do well to heed in the midst of apostolic ministry. What a beautiful picture is painted here.

Authentic apostolic individuals will not have to be summoned by other leadership to come in for dialogue or correction. Rather, they will initiate the opportunity to receive advice, wisdom, and spiritual guidance. They will be disposed toward communication and try to work within the system. This kind of attitude allows for the insight and blessing of others in the Body of Christ which is much better than acting singularly. Paul is such an excellent example of this!

When it comes to prophets and this topic of checks and balances, Scripture often characterizes them as being particularly humble. An example is Moses. Numbers 12:3 says, "Now Moses was a very humble man, more humble than anyone else on the face of the earth." The reticence of authentic prophets to give difficult messages and their pain when people don't listen are further examples of this. They don't allow getting revelation from God to go to their heads.

Staying humble can be a challenge for today's prophetic or apostolic voices. Often, they find themselves isolated with few other contemporaries. Even those in the church can become mesmerized with those who administer the gifts. Thus, a challenge for these men and women is resisting the urge to think they are some of the few who are hearing or speaking for God. Consider Elijah's cry in 1 Kings 19:14, "I am the only one left, and now they are trying to kill me too." But God reminds him there are actually 7,000 left (v.18). In such moments as these, doors may open for pride or arrogance, isolationism, or offense to enter in. The prophetic was meant to be exercised in fellowship with other like-minded people who are desirous of moving in the Spirit. This affords a safety net for prophetic functioning.

1 Corinthians 14:29-33 provides understanding about the overall checks and balances of prophetic ministry:

> Two or three prophets should speak, and the others should weigh carefully what is said. And if a revelation comes to someone who is sitting down, the first speaker should stop. For you can all prophesy in turn so that everyone may be instructed and encouraged. The spirits of prophets are subject to the control of prophets. For God is not a God of disorder but of peace—as in all the congregations of the Lord's people.

Those who work in the prophetic should be connected to others who are called to this function. They are not a "one-man-band," but instead, others are meant to weigh—and not just weigh but weigh carefully—what is said. Prophetic persons should strive to properly discern what God is wanting to say. Their spirits are subject to others who are prophetically sensitive, seeing if they are sensing the same things. Perhaps one will have a little more to add on what another said, thereby providing even more insight or affirmation. This is a security feature for the prophetic individual. The context of what is being said here may sound foreign today, but it worked well in group worship of the Early Church where the prophetic flowed naturally.

The problem is that today, few move in the prophetic, so the drought of spiritual flow automatically brings a lack of proper checks and balances along with it. Those who function in it have the best sense of what is right, and this explains why pastors and others sometimes just aren't sure about something that is said. We will be discussing more about this, but first, let's look at three chapters on just what apostolic functioning specifically looks like, followed by a consideration of prophetic functioning.

Chapter Two

The Basic Work of Apostolicity: Pushing Back the Darkness

*"The light shines in the darkness
and the darkness has not overcome it."*
John 1:5

Even the blackest darkness will not win against the light. God intended that the light of Jesus would continue to shine in all of the darkest places. Apostolicity moves courageously into any enemy-held territory of Satan and sets up a bright outpost where God can bring healing, truth, and freedom. This requires a special empowering and clear direction from the Spirit, but it is God's heart and a primary purpose for the Church.

How exactly does the apostolic operate? What are the basics? Many Christians, frankly, are unable to answer such a question. The reason has nothing to do with intelligence but rather with lack of experience: the apostolic is seldom taught or even discussed. Most church goers could easily write out a job description for a pastor, an evangelist, or a teacher, but the apostolic can seem puzzling. In spite of this, apostolic work occurs in many capacities within the Church; we simply need to become more cognizant of what it entails. This chapter will consider keys to the foundational aspects of apostolicity, while the following chapters will offer more details.

Treading New Territory
While numerous observable apostolic functions exist, probably the most basic one is to take the church into uncharted territory. The

Holy Spirit guides apostolic leaders to pursue what has not been tried, plant where few seeds have been sown, and preach what no one has yet heard.

Those used in apostolicity are innovators in finding new ways to forge hard ground. Alan Johnson summarizes the apostolic dynamic in his book *Apostolic Function in 21st Century Missions*: "Paul's sense of apostleship explicitly included going where Christ was not named and not building on another person's foundation, and finally, his choices of ministry location were guided supernaturally by the Spirit."[10] Johnson believes many modern-day missions programs have lost some of their original focus on unreached people groups, choosing instead to work in places where the gospel has already made significant inroads. Indeed, it is critical not to lose the apostolic focus of going to the edge...to the ends of the earth...to places where no one or few have been saved.

Genuine apostolic thrust into a desolate area is difficult work, and few may come to the Lord initially. But those given to apostolicity do not shy away from proclaiming God's truth in tough circumstances. They challenge obstacles and determine to stand against all odds. The Church can be refreshed in the fact that the Holy Spirit still calls men and women for apostolic function, shifting their present ministry platforms to send them out into a new work.

Apostolic initiatives are on the offensive, including going, pursuing, planting, pushing, and proclaiming. Apostles are apt to be led where Satan previously held reign and darkness is prevailing. Spiritual warfare has always been a symbol of the mission of the Church. It brings clearer focus to the concept of the gates of hell which Jesus told the apostle Peter would never prevail against His church (Matt. 16:18). To "prevail" means to prove more powerful than opposing forces and thereby be victorious.

I (Joe) recently visited various ancient church fortress sites across Israel. Concerning ancient city gates, Amos Millard posits, "The gates of ancient cities were the most vulnerable point of attack in warfare. An invading army would storm the gates to break them down and gain access into the city. Thus, Jesus implied His Church would be on the offensive, not the defensive."[11] Apostolic initiatives are certainly on the offensive and include going, pursuing, challenging, planting, pushing, and proclaiming. The gates of hell will not be able to stand up under this spiritual assault; they will not prevail; they will fall.

The task of apostolic leadership in the Early Church and now is to lead the charge for the Church to advance. God gives the vision of what must be done, the courage to go after it, and the faith in God to sustain the push forward. Those called to the apostolic are clearly emissaries, sent by God to certain places and people groups to accomplish His bidding. This can include geographic locations, new initiatives in ministry, or sometimes daunting efforts into broken relationships. The apostolic task is to push back darkness, pray through, intercede for the people, and do any spiritual warfare necessary until there is a breakthrough and people start getting saved. Apostolicity may well be "the single greatest human threat in existence to the work of Satan."[12]

Boldness

A pronounced example of this push into dark places is recorded in Acts 19 when Paul returned to Ephesus—then a part of Greece and generally thought to be tied with Antioch as the third largest metropolis in the entire Roman Empire. Ephesus was a sophisticated city of commerce where one might anticipate difficulties making Christian inroads, but Paul had a great impact. He preached "boldly" in the synagogue, and after facing opposition, he moved to the hall of Tyrannus where he held discussions daily for two years "so that all the Jews and Greeks who lived in the province of Asia heard the word of the Lord" (Acts 19:10). Think of that! He made such an impression in the whole region that everybody knew about him.

Paul was by no means hidden away as an apostle to the Gentiles. In fact, his presence even upset the economy of Ephesus. Demetrius the silversmith and his business associates were losing sales from their silver shrines of Artemis. The people coming to her temple there (one of the Seven Wonders of the Ancient World and four times the size of the Athenian Parthenon) were apparently being affected by Paul's message and no longer wanted an idol. Demetrius called all the tradespeople together in Acts 19: 26-27 and said this:

"And you see and hear how this fellow Paul has convinced and led astray large numbers of people here in Ephesus and in practically the whole province of Asia. He says that gods made by human hands are no gods at all. There is danger not only that our trade will lose its good name, but also that the temple of the great goddess Artemis will be discredited; and the goddess herself, who is worshiped throughout the province of Asia and the world, will be robbed of her divine majesty."

Well, of course, this was exactly Paul's agenda; the walls of this pagan religion were crumbling.

Apostolically he was "taking on" the darkness of this entire territory and was desirous of bringing it to nothing less than collapse. Demetrius and the angry mob seized some of Paul's traveling companions, and the riot spilled into the massive theater that seated 25,000 people.

Both of us (Joe and Carolyn) have had opportunities to be at this theater, still in existence today in modern-day Turkey. It has almost perfect acoustics. A person can literally hear a pin drop on the other side of the theater. The noise of a rioting mob in that place would have been a fearsome thing indeed, but Paul wanted to go into the middle of the very riot which was incited against him! This indicates the boldness of an apostle, the assurance one called by God is going to be victorious over any odds. Here you see the epitome of the apostolic spirit.

Years ago, during early pastoral ministry, I (Joe) became deeply burdened over matters of spiritual-warfare arising within the church's worship team regularly leading our growing congregation. After nearly a year of personal and prayerful battles, I sensed the Lord was asking me to take a bold stand against the stronghold of disunity that the enemy had wedged, now deeply and adversely impacting the ministry. Calling together all the musicians and singers, I explained from my written notes that though I knew few if any would understand this move, as pastor I had decided to sit down the entire worship team for a period of one year. Those who chose to stay with the church during that time would be asked to reconsider joining in music ministry again. In the meantime, I would have to rely upon the Lord to help develop another plan for music and worship over the course of the twelve months ahead.

The move—challenging beyond what can be described at this juncture—proved a year later to be one of the paramount decisions of my pastorate and to date of my ministry history. Of course, many challenges had to be dealt with during this ordeal. But, within the next years to come, as God touched all our hearts and nearly all of the original team members returned to their ministries, a previously unseen unity bound us together for an unprecedented move of God and divine favor in the church. Now, years later, most of those same individuals, initially hurt, angry, confused, and ministry-displaced because of this pastor's sense of hearing from the Lord, are incredibly respected, loved, and trusted personal friends for life.

The apostles had spent time in God's presence, and His mantle accompanied the work.

Boldness of this nature was a mark of early apostles. In Acts 3, Peter and John healed a lame beggar outside of the temple. This created such a stir that they were thrown into prison for the night and then called before the Sanhedrin. But Peter spoke out fearlessly, and the Sanhedrin reacted in Acts 4:13: "When they saw the courage of Peter and John and realized that they were unschooled, ordinary men, they were astonished and they took note that these men had been with Jesus." The apostles had spent time in God's presence learning what He desired of them, and the apostolic mantle of authority accompanied the work.

When told to stop speaking and teaching in the name of Jesus, Peter and John said, "Oh, so sorry we have bothered you, and we will keep quiet from now on." Oh, no. Of course not! They were not intimidated to stop sharing about Jesus. They said, "As for us, we cannot help speaking about what we have seen and heard." A boldness from the Holy Spirit was apparent to all. They were apostles, called, anointed, and propelled by the Spirit to go and share what Jesus had done for all mankind.

When delivered from this experience the Sanhedrin had designed to frighten and weaken them, Peter and John joined the church people who started strategizing and talking about what they should do. Is that right? Again, no. They immediately prayed! Acts 4:29-31 records this ending to their prayer:

> "Now, Lord, consider their threats and enable your servants to speak your word with great boldness. Stretch out your hand to heal and

perform signs and wonders through the name of your holy servant Jesus."

After they prayed, the place where they were meeting was shaken. And they were all filled with the Holy Spirit and spoke the word of God boldly.

The authors don't remember ever hearing a prayer for boldness in our churches anywhere. It is not a common wish. But perhaps this is evidence of how far we have come from an apostolic yearning and flow in our churches today. We are in great need of going back to our Pentecostal roots which shook people to their core and released a courageous boldness and God-given authority.

Daniel Henderson says, "By New Testament measurements, we are anemic and shallow. We certainly are distracted. Could it be we are powerless at the very moment when our society needs to experience the reality of faith that rests on the power of God and not the wisdom of men?" (See 1 Cor. 2:5).[13]

The Early Church Advanced Through Apostolic Leadership
The Early Church advanced because the apostolic functioning was surging strongly through the power of the Holy Spirit. The Church added 3,000 people on the day of Pentecost alone and increased daily after that (Acts 2:47). In Acts 4 there were 5,000 men who were saved after Peter and John healed the lame man and were thrown into prison. The ensuing chapters tell of the groups of believers swelling rapidly—with signs and wonders evident—and repeatedly describe the steady growth of the Church, often by scores of people at a time (Acts 5:14; 6:1,7; 9:31; 11:21-26 to name a few).

The apostolic pushes to the edges and corners of greatest need where Satan is having a heyday.

After Paul and Barnabas were "sent off" by the Antioch church in Acts 13, they went to Seleucia and Cyprus where the proconsul believed, then on to Pisidian Antioch and then Iconium where they spoke "so effectively" in the Jewish synagogue that a "great number of Jews and Gentiles believed" (14:1). Paul and Barnabas also went to Derbe where they "preached the good news" and "won a large number of disciples" (v. 21). Later, Paul, Timothy, and Silas traveled from town to town, and the "churches were strengthened in the faith and grew daily in

The Basic Work of Apostilicy: Pushing Back the Darkness

numbers" (16:5). In Berea Paul preached, and here "[m]any of the Jews believed, as did also a number of prominent Greek women and many Greek men" (Acts 17: 12).

The apostolic function pushes to the edge, to the corners with the greatest needs and the out-of-way places where Satan is having a heyday. Early apostles traveled extensively and seemed to have flexibility and innovation from the Lord in handling each situation and the many new converts. Although they did not neglect sharing the message with the Jews, they were able to head further into unfamiliar territory, places that were dark—full of paganism and idolatry. They received extraordinary wisdom from God about how to act and speak in these pagan cultures. Remember Paul's discourse on Mars Hill in Athens, right next to the Parthenon? In the midst of the idols, God gave Paul insight on effectively contextualizing the gospel message.

Even before this, back when the Apostles were being trained by Jesus, He dispatched seventy, two-by-two, giving them power and authority to expand His Father's Kingdom. They were sent to "every town and place where he was about to go" (Luke 10:1). This would break up fallow ground in the hearts of men and women, and the healing of the sick and casting out of demons would awaken the people to the coming of Jesus Himself. It can be this way still today before the second coming of Christ.

When the seventy returned, Jesus said, "I saw Satan fall like lightning from heaven. I have given you authority to trample on snakes and scorpions and to overcome all the power of the enemy; nothing will harm you" (v. 18-19). Though they were strong in the spiritual battle, He didn't want them caught in any misuse of power so He immediately added, "However, do not rejoice that the spirits submit to you, but rejoice that your names are written in heaven" (v. 20).

Anybody working in the apostolic must be ready to face the darkness of Satan and the world of sin. This is not a task for the faint of heart. If Satan has previously held certain territory, he does not wish to turn that ground back over to God as people become disciples of Jesus and the church is established. There will be a fight. In our experience, quite a few who are called to apostolicity today are not prepared for the kick-back from Satan.

When I (Joe) entered the ministry, I had no idea, nor was it ever addressed in seminary, that I would be sued or need a personal attorney. Now, over three decades into the ministry journey and having been sued numerous times, I have the cell and office phone numbers of more than one attorney at my disposal. Ministry, even for those pure in heart, will have conflict and kick-back from the devil himself. Those called to apostolicity will have to overcome spiritual attacks.

Further, it is imperative to acknowledge that those working in the apostolic are not always completely aware of their own anointing or the spiritual mantle upon them. Neither do some fully use the authority Christ has given them. This is why certain apostolic projects ultimately fail.

Any breakdown of apostolic establishment is not merely a lack in those called to the apostolic. Rather it is also the dearth of prayer and intercession on the part of the sending church—prayer which is so greatly needed if the battle is to be won. Leonard Ravenhill said, "Prayer is not a preparation for the battle; it is the battle!"[14] Will we all join in and pick up our share of the effort? Do we really care? Will we pray?

For the church to advance, those functioning in the apostolic must stand up in their role, and simultaneously the church needs to provide stronger support. Jim Cymbala said, "Thirty minutes of Spirit-aided intercessory prayer is more effective than all the new programs and stylistic changes we are constantly tinkering with. Human ingenuity cannot be compared to God's power."[15] We need to be involved in prayer support as we battle the spiritual forces if apostolicity is to make inroads and impact.

Modern Day Examples of Apostolicity

Just as the Early Church moved ahead through the work of the apostles and of the caring and supportive churches who sent them, this is still the model for apostolic functioning today. We must move into the darkness and establish the Church in areas where it does not exist or is weak. This task remains enormous. There is certainly no lack of places to go or people to reach. The population continues to expand, and so many people have yet to hear the good news and become strong disciples.

Understanding what apostolicity entails will assist the Church in recognizing how God is leading, so let's consider some of the contemporary roles that are likely to be apostolic in nature.

While some missionaries serve as teachers or pastors, most missionaries are involved in apostolic leadership. This role began with early missionaries like Paul, Barnabas, and others sent to places that did not have an established witness. As soon as the church was founded there, they left it in the hands of pastors, teachers, prophets, and evangelists to carry on, moving to a new location where they laid the foundation for another life-giving church. This is why Ephesians 2:20 speaks of God's household being "built on the foundation of the apostles and prophets, with Jesus Christ Himself as the chief cornerstone." The apostolic task—along with the prophets—was to lay the basic foundation of the Church, and we certainly witness this in New Testament writings.

Today people still accomplish foundational functions. In missions they institute churches, Bible schools, orphanages and other programs and outreaches too numerous to name. Missionaries move into unreached people groups and establish a newborn church. They train national believers, equipping them for the work of ministry in their own territory. As the local church matures, indigenous leaders accept these tasks and likewise become apostolic by planting more churches in their country, establishing fresh inroads, equipping recent converts and their leaders, and in turn, sending out their own missionaries to foreign lands.

Missionary workers also spend time hosting mission trips composed of teams from various churches or schools. This is an opportunity for members of a team to expand their apostolic perspective, to participate in meeting needs outside of the local church, and to gain cross-cultural skills which can transfer to their home contexts. Mission trips also allow potential future missionaries to see first-hand what apostolic work actually entails and to open up to their own call. The trips unveil needs, wake people up to economic disparity, and encourage generosity. In this way, apostolic missionaries are "equipping the people for works of service" (Eph. 5:12) as they are called to do. A missionary to a closed country whom I (Carolyn) met with this week talked about how teams open doors that wouldn't normally be provided. Towns and local institutions are willing to host visitors and are prepared for them to be cross-culturally different, affording more freedom of ministry than normal.

Although numerous examples are available of effective apostolic work on the foreign mission field, a great illustration is John L. Franklin. In 1937 he took his new wife, Ella, along with very few belongings to Guatemala and secured a mule to get to five small congregations previously established in the mountains. The Franklins moved around to each group, sleeping in hammocks, bathing in mountains streams, struggling with illness, drinking unsafe water, dealing with swarms of mosquitoes and fleas, and eating mainly beans and tortillas. Each church was given a territory and taught to do their own evangelization and church planting, thereby establishing an apostolic culture. In 1941, Franklin opened a church in Guatemala City with mostly children, but on Good Friday a revival sparked and a large, well-attended evangelistic center resulted. When they retired forty years after coming to Guatemala, there were 600 churches, 700 licensed ministers, and 55,000 Assemblies of God believers.[16]

In the United States, most home missionaries also carry a significant apostolic role. Many reach people with special needs including the deaf, blind, handicapped, addicted, orphaned, and the trafficked. They work with Native Americans including Alaskans, cowboys and others on the rodeo circuit, along with ministries to Hispanics, Asians, cults, Muslims, Russians/Slavs, Jews, and the list goes on. Home missionary work also encompasses ministry with college and university students as well as a vast group of chaplains in the military, hospitals, prisons, and the marketplace. Each of these are critical for God's Kingdom to be extended.

Church planters must be prepared for the battle Satan is waging in that territory.

Church planters should likewise have an apostolic calling. They are laying a foundation where there has previously been inadequate church presence. While there are varying reasons for a church plant to falter, often it is because planters were unprepared for the battle Satan would wage for that territory. Being successful at church planting is not about following man-made strategies, though learning does not hurt. What is most important is how God wants to grow His church. As apostolic church planters humbly bow before God, He will direct them and show them what to do. There is no short cut for this.

Planters should not miss the critical element of secret place intimacy with God in prayer.

I (Carolyn) remember once having a mission team in Argentina. We visited a church where thousands of people attended in 21 services a week. The evangelist for this church told us they had a baptismal service once every three months, and they were baptizing 500 people that week. We met with the pastor who shared about the church, and then we were able to ask questions. Someone on the team queried, "Do you have all this written up? A manual or something like that?" I cringed.

The pastor put his head down and waited for a bit. Then he said, "I get asked that question all the time by visitors. I have never said this before, but I have always wanted to. No, I don't have a manual, and I never will. You have to grow your church the way I grew this one. Get on your face and seek God for what He has for you. There is no shortcut to this. The Lord has plans, and you have to discover what those are. They won't be listed in anybody else's manual." God has unique ways for growing His church in different locales. We must learn directly from Him what He has in mind.

Apostolic thinking needs to be woven into the warp and weft of the fiber of any church.

In September of 1992, at thirty years of age, I (Joe) accepted the call and became a lead pastor. Soon the need for developing prayer in the church riddled with challenges was high on my agenda. Initially, as many pastors witness, few would join me in prayer. Sometime later, it was a victory when two or more of the church's board members would choose to come to a specially called prayer meeting. Then, over time, as many as eighty people were registered to pray and fast weekly, some all night, others for hourly schedules around the clock. And, during one of the most amazing seasons of ministry where we were seeing people come to Christ and being baptized in water weekly as a normal part of our Sunday service, there were dozens who gathered in a prayer room each Sunday morning while I was preaching the Word. As I had instructed, they simply prayed I wouldn't mess up that day and that God would have His way to meet needs, change lives, and restore relationships. That wasn't in a manual. It was simply God-ordained, and it made the difference for the ministry as people heard from God for themselves about how to advance the church.

Church planters should not simply be establishing a local congregation that takes care of itself, but also one which reaches out and functions apostolically in its own community and abroad. If this design is part of the founding vision of a new church, from the beginning it will be comfortable with operating in fresh ways to move beyond itself. Apostolic thinking needs to be woven into the warp and weft of the fiber of any church. I recently spoke with the pastor of a small church that is being revitalized. She said they just made the decision to tithe on the income of the church in supporting missionaries. This is a sacrifice since there are many needs, but the church is now learning various ways of moving outside of themselves and thinking apostolically.

Besides church planters, other roles for the apostolic include district and denominational leadership who should be aware of and acquiesce to their apostolic calling in order to function well. Their very job responsibilities follow the apostolic responsibilities described in this book, and to try to carry out these weighty requirements without accepting the anointing and mantle from God makes the position far more difficult than it needs to be.

Likely within the setting of the local church there are also many functioning with apostolic gifts. They may be unacknowledged and remain unaccounted for simply because the church's leadership may not realize how to identify the apostolic gifting set. They often come up with ideas to make inroads into the local community through different sorts of creative programming and outreach.

Also included in apostolicity are those who work with groups that interconnect various denominations within a city, a region, a state, a county, or among various nations are often apostolic. Those who have founded such movements as the following were sent by the Lord to meet a particular need and extend the Kingdom of God: Chi Alpha, Youth for Christ, Teen Challenge, Project Rescue, the Navigators, InterVarsity Christian Fellowship, Youth with a Mission (YWAM), the Fellowship of Christian Athletes, Promise Keepers, L'Abri Fellowship, Focus on the Family, Student Venture, Acts in Africa (AIA), the National Association of Evangelicals, Oral Language Initiative (ORI), Walk Thru the Bible, Mercy Ships,

Unsion, ADtv, Young Life, Royal Family Kids Camps, Special Forces, World Relief, and Convoy of Hope. These groups all have clear apostolic outcomes.

The Cost of Serving Apostolically

Among these contemporary apostolic roles, high costs are often paid to make advances. From the beginning, apostolic labor has never been easy. Difficulties, challenges, set-backs, and attacks from the enemy are common as shown in the New Testament and in the testimonies of apostolic workers today. As a matter of fact, another apostolic sign—and an expected part of the job description—includes bearing up under suffering and persecution. This should not be surprising since Satan is still active.

Authentic apostolic workers are willing to serve, even if they must pay a great price.

Although terrible to experience, God often seems to use persecution as a divine opportunity to spread the gospel. The apostles all endured suffering, but the Lord was in the middle of the circumstances (see 2 Cor. 4:7-18). Every time the apostles were driven away to a new location, that place became another opportunity.

In 2 Corinthians 11:16-33 and 12:1-13, Paul chronicled some of his sufferings, persecutions, insults, weaknesses, church burdens, and pressures. We can spot authentic apostolic workers. They're willing to serve even though they are likely to pay a great price. Paul specifically, according to his own list of hazards, was often thrown into prison, flogged severely, exposed to death repeatedly, beaten with rods, and pelted with stones. He was shipwrecked three days and spent a night and a day in open sea. He was constantly on the move. Danger was everywhere: from rivers, bandits, his own fellow Jews, the Gentiles, from false believers and in both city and country as well as at sea. He labored and toiled, often without sleep, enduring both hunger and thirst. Then there was his concern for all the churches and the many problems he needed to straighten out with them, even when he wasn't present. He was pained when people turned back from following Jesus or were led into sin; it caused him tangible grief. This is more than a story; it was real life for him.

Paul says he was a fool to write down all these negatives, but it is good for history that he did. Those called to apostolic service must not take the call lightly. They should be prepared for what comes their way, determining they will be strong in the Lord, even in the midst of personal weakness. Apostolicity is not a calling for the faint-hearted.

Roland Allen pointed out, "In arriving at a decision in a question of doubt, the apostles in the Acts were guided solely by their sense of the Spirit behind the action, not by any speculations as to consequences which might ensue. And so they found the truth."[17]

Apostolicity requires dying to self...to individual desires, comfortability, securities, pleasures, and accolades. Instead, troubles, misunderstandings, conflict, burdens, and "junk" are likely to come in their place. There will be no shortage of critics, and decisions can't be made based upon whether people will like it. Apostolic workers will probably toil till they drop, but it will never seem to be enough, and most people won't appreciate it.

Those called and anointed for the apostolic will keep running the race, no matter how difficult it becomes. Eckhardt writes, "Instead of stopping apostles, persecution stirs them; it fuels their ministries."[18]

Someone directly or unconsciously expecting honor, position, and title will abandon the real apostolic operation. Oh, they might keep the title and position, but they will squirm out of the "dirty work," avoiding it, assigning it to others, or looking the other way. They will sidestep accountability and instead bask in the public eye as the leader they've created themselves to be. Remember that many before us have run a very difficult apostolic race and managed to finish it well. This should be an encouragement to stay strong in the Lord and remain on the offensive.

The Importance of Signs and Wonders

One of the strongest offensive weapons for apostolic advancement is moving in signs, wonders, and miracles. God uses these, along with prayer, to make apostolic inroads. Through them, unbelievers can see for themselves that God wields more power than Satan. He is surely the One deserving allegiance. Apostolic work shows, not just tells. It demonstrates God's power, grace, and love and makes them virtually observable. Signs and wonders attract people to Jesus, and they "authenticate... preaching, remove hindrances, draw people to faith, ensure the gospel's effectiveness, and bring glory to God."[19]

Apostolic work shows, not just tells.

On-going references to miracles, signs, and wonders interfuse the Acts narrative of the constantly expanding Early Church: Peter raised Dorcas from the dead, and Paul raised Eutychus; prison doors swung open; people were translated to a different place; they spoke in other tongues; demons were cast out; so many received physical healings. Throughout Acts, miraculous signs and wonders are mentioned continuously, and the result usually was that there was a "stir." People came to the Lord, and the Church was established and advanced.

God used the apostles in these miracles. Jesus Christ, as the chief cornerstone of the Church, performed miracles, signs, and wonders as a model for us to follow, and He prophesied that the miracles would continue. In John 14:11-14, Jesus said this:

> "Believe me when I say that I am in the Father and the Father is in me; or at least believe on the evidence of the works themselves. Very truly I tell you, whoever believes in me will do the works I have been doing, and they will do even greater things than these, because I am going to the Father. And I will do whatever you ask in my name, so that the Father may be glorified in the Son. You may ask me for anything in my name, and I will do it."

Jesus said "whoever" believes in Him would do the works He was doing and even greater things. God clearly wants to use us in demonstrating His love and goodness through healings, deliverance, and miracles today. When unbelievers see signs and wonders, they suddenly realize the power of the Lord, and their eyes open to His greatness. They become persuaded God Himself is so much greater than the inadequate idols and philosophies they have been serving. The realization dawns upon them that God is able to break the power of sin, save them from their addictions, heal their bodies and their minds, and totally set them free! Anything else offers a gospel of weak broth.

Paul refers to his own documentation as a genuine apostle when he states, "I persevered in demonstrating among you the marks of a true apostle, including signs, wonders and miracles" (2 Cor. 12:12). These signs are an important point for anyone called to the apostolic role. It accompanied all those whom Jesus sent out, and it can and should still accompany those today. For the ones who have an apostolic calling, missing the miraculous does not mean they are not called, but rather that they have more praying to do regarding this matter.

Signs, wonders and miracles show God's power. Anything else offers a gospel of weak broth.

Anyone seeking to learn more about the divine healing power of God for today would be encouraged by reading more testimonies of healing miracles. One place to find this is Dr. Craig Keener's extensive two-volume set *Miracles*[20] offering researched hundreds of contemporary healings along with the theologian's own expertise regarding the credibility of the New Testament accounts of the miraculous. Another option is to check out books on the history of Church revivals.

Since we are God's emissaries, His agents for good on this earth, we must remember that others will understand God according to how we act. If we behave like weaklings, shallow representatives of the faith, they will see God as such. If we cannot pray in faith with expectation, believing God can set people free from their sin and addictions, they will erroneously arrive at the conclusion that He is not able to break these chains. If they do not witness miracles and divine-favor in the lives of those proclaiming apostolicity and prophetic giftings, they may shun faith in the truth.

Apostolic leaders for the modern Church must prepare to function in the various gifts of the Spirit and in miracles, signs, and wonders, as did the New Testament apostles. The God-given ability to minister physical, spiritual, or emotional healing to those in need accompanies the apostolic gifting. The working of miracles did not cease with the death of the New Testament apostles. The continuity of apostolic function is assured by the fact that no scriptural evidence exists for cessation of the gifts. The manifestation of supernatural acts is prevalent in the modern Church, widespread in witness and testimony (especially among Pentecostal and Charismatic circles globally) and available for all Spirit-empowered leaders.

Chapter Three

Work Details for Apostolicity

*"The wall of the city had twelve foundations,
and on them were the names of the twelve apostles of the Lamb."*
Revelation 21:14

The early first- and second-century Church understood the functions of apostolicity. They grasped the new concept of the Church being built upon the foundation of the apostles and prophets. Unique from prophets, pastors, teachers, and evangelists, references to the word *apostle* are mentioned at least eighty-three times in the New Testament. *Apostle* is used as a noun nineteen times, in plural forms sixty times, and *apostleship* is used four times.[21]

New Testament apostles were visionaries with the Spirit-led purpose of initiating, establishing, and developing the work of the Church. Certainly, there is diversity in apostolic calling,[22] and not all New Testament apostles fit the same mold in relation to their individual gifts. Still, each fulfilled the Spirit-empowered character and calling to accomplish their tasks.

The following table provides a summary of some of the biblical characteristics and ministry of those with apostolic function. After looking at this general overview, we will select a few of the job details of apostolicity to discuss more in depth.

Ministry Traits of New Testament Apostles	Scriptural Reference
They are Spirit-filled leaders.	Acts 2:4
They are preachers/proclaimers of the good news.	Acts 2:14ff
They are used in the ministry of healing.	Acts 3:1-8
They are accustomed to being persecuted, even martyred.	Acts 4:1ff, 12:1
They are not timid to speak judgment.	Acts 5:1ff, 13:11 w
They perform signs and wonders/miracles, even the raising of the dead.	Acts 5:12, 9:36ff
Their sole topic of ministry/preaching is Jesus Christ.	Acts 5:42
They ordain deacons of the Church, ministers of the faith, elders.	Acts 6:1ff, 14:23
They are used in the laying on of hands.	Acts 8:14-17
They plant and initiate new churches and ministries, send other ministers to do the same, and set churches in order.	Acts 8ff, 19:22; 1 Cor. 11:34
They preach the message of Jesus where it has not gone before, to the Gentiles.	Acts 10
They are called and sent by the Holy Spirit, not themselves nor man.	Acts 13:4
They teach doctrinal purity and settle doctrinal disagreements.	Acts 15:1ff
They use God's power to cast out demons.	Acts 16:18
They serve as counselors to those in the Church.	1 Cor. 7:11
They care for the churches and their needs.	2 Cor. 11:28
They expend their influence for edification.	2 Cor. 13:10
They are predominantly establishers of the faith.	Eph. 2:20

Training and Maturing the Church

Jesus proclaimed the five gifts of Ephesians 4:11 as highlighted necessities for the establishment and growth of His Church. These were His presents to the Church after His victory over Satan, and they provided the keys for how the Church could become what He intended. The context of verses 8-10 refers to the victory of ancient war generals when they came home and paraded through the city with their captives, doling out the collected wealth and loot as cherished gifts and rewards to their captains and soldiers.[23] Jesus won the victory and doled out to the church five precious gifts designed to be great treasures. Certainly, we should never take lightly His largesse purchased at such a great price. The gifts benefit the entire Church.

Leaders functioning in any of these five gifts have substantial duties as God-called servants of Jesus Christ. A short study of the Ephesians passage (4:11-13) provides important perspective on these responsibilities:

> So Christ himself gave the apostles, the prophets, the evangelists, the pastors and teachers, to equip his people for works of service, so that the body of Christ may be built up until we all reach unity in the faith and in the knowledge of the Son of God and become mature, attaining to the whole measure of the fullness of Christ.

Paul unmistakably states the work of ministry is to be carried out by all believers. Those functioning as evangelists, pastors, teachers, and in apostolic and prophetic roles have certain prescribed tasks. The assignment all of them have is to equip the believers to perform these five services. In their relationship to the church, the leaders are not to rule over others. On the contrary, their role is specifically to train other members of the church to participate in, support, pray for, and value the five main ministry functions.

Any time apostolic workers visit a church, for example, they should stir up interest in apostolic expansion, encouraging the local church to reach beyond their church building. They need not announce their own arrival or proclaim their apostleship. Their actions and teaching speak for themselves. Missionaries need sufficient time to share their work so the church will pray and support apostolic undertaking. They should equip the church members to serve others in their own communities. Apostolicity must be in the flow of the entire Church.

Commitment to apostolicity helps the church reach unity of purpose and gain a broader picture of what God is doing around the world. The church will become interested in different people groups, grow in appreciation of diversity, and expand compassion for the needs of others. They will learn more about Jesus Himself and His love for people, His concerns for justice, and His yearning to set humanity free from Satan's chains. A church that does not care about apostolic growth will become ingrown, declining, and self-centered. Apostolicity leads the church to maturity and Christocentric focus on the Lord's heart for the world. It will help them not to act like self-absorbed children, but rather look toward the grander scheme of God's great Kingdom—to push out beyond themselves and see the needs God wants them to meet outside their church walls.

Demonstrating Maturity

In order to lead the Church to maturity, those teaching must personally model what living as a mature Christian actually looks like. Anyone involved in apostolicity needs to evidence the same traits as New Testament apostles.

First of all, this involves a yearning for the presence of God and spending time in His presence in prayer. Just as Christ prioritized prayer and taught his disciples/apostles to do so, this is a *sine qua non* for us today. Jesus and His disciples desired to hear what God expected of them. They moved from place to place based upon His clear direction, and they accomplished His work. Apostolicity in today's local church provides both purpose and boundaries as the Holy Spirit reveals strategies and directives.

The contemporary Church must not only pray for personal guidance but also for other churches, leaders, and those being equipped to do the work of service. Certainly, Jesus made praying for His disciples a significant part of His routine (John 17:6-19). Jesus' commitment to others was a paradigm shift from the world's standard: "Greater love has no one than this, to lay down one's life for one's friends. You are my friends if you do what I command" (John 15:13-14). Apostolic functions in today's church generally require Spirit-empowered teams driven by genuine love, prayer, and dedication to God and one another.

After Jesus' ascension, the apostles and others prayed and

waited for days in God's presence to receive direction and empowerment from the Holy Spirit, a clear requirement for the effective apostolic work which followed. They were obeying Jesus' direction to wait in Jerusalem until they were "clothed with power from on high" (Luke 24:49). Anyone serving in church leadership today needs the empowerment which comes through the baptism in the Holy Spirit.

Having been reared in a strict Southern Baptist home, I (Joe) was little exposed at an early age to the scriptures and doctrines of Spirit baptism and full-gospel ministries. A few months after a radical experience with the Lord while in college which still did not include the baptism in the Holy Spirit, I was convinced I knew the girl I would someday marry. I had never met her personally; I had only seen her from a distance at the church I had chosen to attend. Asking her out on a first date proved providential as she said she would never marry a man not baptized in the Spirit. That sealed the deal. I began to read scripture, study, and pray until I found and experienced what the Lord had been offering all along...and I did marry her.

We shouldn't be in a hurry to leave the King's presence—the secret place.

The baptism in the Holy Spirit provides power to witness, a flow of the gifts of the Spirit through a person's life and ministry, and sensitivity to the Spirit's work. It also sharpens a deep desire for God's Word, another necessity for apostolicity. Peter 2:2 speaks of spiritual hunger for the Word by using the picture of newborn babies longing for pure milk to help them grow. Jesus said in John 8:31 that those who heed His word are His true disciples. Therefore, the New Testament shows us how Spirit-empowered leaders not only hear but live for and yearn after the things of God. From a list of fifty things learned in ministry, I (Joe) often address the matter of not being in a hurry to leave the King's presence—the secret place.

Apostolicity requires strong inclinations of faith. It demands Spirit-directed desire for new initiatives and witness endeavors, having shifted from wanting a visitation from God to longing for a habitation of God—an abiding presence shaping, molding, and establishing every experience in Christ. Holy Spirit-involved elements are found in every dimension of the church's endeavors. The Spirit invests in leaders by using their faith in God's Word to do supernatural works for the Kingdom.

No doubt, research of apostolic leadership in the New Testament offers strength to the preaching of God's Word and the imperative to continue until He returns. This is a paramount duty of those called to the apostolic, but it demands deep knowledge and insight into the Word as well as the enabling of the Holy Spirit.

The Greek word *apophthengomai* used in both verses 2 and 14 of Acts 2 indicates that the Spirit "enabled" speaking in tongues on the day of Pentecost, and then He "enabled" Peter who spontaneously preached to the crowd that had gathered. This Greek verb speaks of prophetic inspiration which was a result of enablement by the Holy Spirit. Spirit-filled apostolic preachers speak from God and their message is effective, as seen on the day of Pentecost when thousands were saved. Paul was also aware of the Spirit's enabling when he said, "My message and my preaching were not with wise and persuasive words, but with a demonstration of the Spirit's power" (1 Cor. 2:4).

Spirit-inspired preaching and teaching of the gospel take church leaders to multiple cities, nations, and geographical/missional contexts regularly. Paul, likewise, had a geographical territory which he traversed with some degree of systematic determination on behalf of the gospel message he proclaimed.

Besides prayer, delving into the Word, and waiting on God for direction, insight, and empowerment, the apostolic role also requires strong moral commitment and mature personal traits. This includes exhibiting the fruit of the Spirit. Besides developing a godly character, all Christian leaders must determine to maintain personal purity and be above reproach in all things so they stand as a model to other believers and to the world. The Prophet Daniel purposed in his heart not to defile himself. It is personal. It is a commitment. It is a spiritual virtue (Daniel 1:8). Holiness must be a paramount longing and aspiration. Casting vision for a holy standard brings tangible transformation. Standards do not always entail rules of legalism but, set by genuine apostolic leaders, they become banners of Spirit-led living and witness. The Christian testimony should be untarnished when compared to the world's values.

Guarding The Church's DNA

The apostolic has a continuity from the original foundation laid by the apostles as we stay faithful to the Scriptures, celebrate the sacraments instituted by Christ and practiced by the apostles, and continue to maintain the proclamation of the gospel to all mankind.

The forging out of correct doctrine and the guardianship of the gospel's core beliefs are a significant responsibility of apostolic function. The Church needs leaders watchful and thorough in finding any digression from the truth. Look at Paul's strong comment in Galatians 1:6-9:

> I am astonished that you are so quickly deserting the one who called you to live in the grace of Christ and are turning to a different gospel—which is really no gospel at all. Evidently some people are throwing you into confusion and are trying to pervert the gospel of Christ. But even if we or an angel from heaven should preach a gospel other than the one we preached to you, let them be under God's curse! As we have already said, so now I say again: If anybody is preaching to you a gospel other than what you accepted, let them be under God's curse!

The New Testament apostles strove to retain proper doctrine in the churches.

You can't get any clearer than that. Paul fought for the maintenance of the true and undistorted message of the gospel. The New Testament apostles strove to retain proper doctrine in the churches. Paul's letters are full of this doctrinal guidance—sometimes reemphasizing certain truths, others times setting straight misguided doctrine and behavior. He was willing to correct, using his shepherd's rod and staff when necessary. Leaders who close their eyes to such problems do not help the pure gospel advance but rather opt for tainting, maintenance, and at best man-empowered efforts far short of God's favored destiny.

In 1 Corinthians 4:18-21, Paul refers to a hassle he has heard about:

> Some of you have become arrogant, as if I were not coming to you. But I will come to you very soon, if the Lord is willing, and then I will find out not only how these arrogant people are talking, but what power they have. For the kingdom of God is not a matter of talk but of power. What do you prefer? Shall I come to you with a rod of discipline, or shall I come in love and with a gentle spirit?

Obviously, Paul did not want to come with an authoritative "rod," but he knew apostleship required bringing correction if necessary, and he would do it if required. Paul's letters are full of these corrections. In 1 Corinthians 11:17-34 he straightens out some serious misuse of the sacrament of the Lord's Supper. He provides guidance regarding the use of the spiritual gifts and the need to bring order into worship services where the Spirit is moving but people are getting out of hand. (1 Cor. 14).

Often the apostles answered questions about what was right and wrong, some of the issues being difficult to decipher in light of contemporary perspectives. These included such concerns as meat sacrificed to idols (1 Cor. 8:1-13) as well as problems created when some claimed there was no resurrection from the dead (1 Cor. 15).

Paul and other church leaders discussed how to settle inevitable issues when both Gentiles and Jews came together in the Church, thus blending Jewish tradition such as circumcision with Christ's message of grace to the Gentiles (Acts 15). This chapter makes it apparent these issues were decided by the "apostles and elders" (v. 4, 6, 22-23), thus incorporating local church leadership in the decision-making. Note that prophecies and prophets also had a part (v. 15-18, 32).

Issues were decided by the apostles and local church elders together.

Although Christ's apostles were strong leaders, when it came to handling doctrinal and practical problems in the churches, they often modeled shared leadership. Dunn makes an important point: "Apostolic authority is exercised not over the Christian community, but within it; and the authority is exercised...'to equip the saints for the work of their ministry, for the building up of Christ's body.'"(Eph. 4:12).[24]

Paul's challenges of moral sorting are still prevalent in today's post-Christian society as church leaders grapple with erroneous doctrines of those who proclaim happiness over holiness, tolerance over truth, or the beliefs of universalism (all will get into heaven).

Since one of the purposes of the five leadership gifts (Eph. 4:13) is to bring the Church to maturity, Paul includes learning the difference between correct and incorrect doctrine. He states, "Then we will no longer be infants, tossed back and forth by the waves, and blown here and there by every wind of teaching and by the cunning and craftiness of people in their deceitful scheming" (v. 14). Over thirty years of pastoral and denominational leadership has proven to me (Joe) how much this mirrors so many leaders and Christ-followers who are tossed around from one fad to another as whims of doctrine, the latest book or conference, and the most popular word of the culture directs their agenda!

Besides doctrine, the apostles concerned themselves with moral issues and preached the necessity of maintaining holiness in an immoral world. These included clear corrections regarding incest (1 Cor. 5), sexual immorality (1 Cor. 6:12-20), and being unequally yoked to unbelievers (2 Cor. 5:14-18). Apostolic leaders must face off against moral drift.

Apostolicity combats the impact of secular humanism upon today's Church, guarding against the impingement of contemporary philosophies upon the scriptural foundation. N. T. Wright states, "Secularism is a complex phenomenon, but it has become a dominant motif of western culture, particularly in the United States."[25] We can choose to live optimistically, however, believing for the Church to impact and change society. While some may worry about infrastructure, preservation, and the world's effect on the Church, Kingdom-minded individuals will focus their concerns on how the Church can further influence society and the world at large.

As Jeff Leake states, "God's values are countercultural. They go against the grain."[26] Thankfully there are many who are willing to strive for this hope, to be different, to fight for a spiritual breakthrough with the fullness of the five-fold gifts advancing the Church as Christ intended.

Apostolicity moves ahead to guard the DNA of the Church, repairing and strengthening the core moral and doctrinal foundation established by the apostles. It pursues proactive ways for the Church to communicate truth. Apostolic leaders seek the wisdom of God—not just the wisdom of the world. 1 Cor. 3:18-19 says, "Do not deceive yourselves. If any of you think you are wise by the standards of this age, you should become 'fools' so that you may become wise. For the wisdom of this world is foolishness in God's sight." It is impossible to effectively combat worldly perspectives without God's wisdom and methods, but thankfully these are available resources.

We find a key to maintaining the Church's DNA in Acts 2:42: "They devoted themselves to the apostles' teaching..." Peter recognized that deceptive societal philosophies and skewed church doctrine challenge the very claim of apostolic authority. If we are to build a strong church able to stand against moral and doctrinal drift, we need to be "devoted" to teaching and peel back deception. We do not need fluffy, self-help sermons. These produce Christian weaklings who themselves will barely be able to stand firm, let alone lead others into the truth. In the midst of it all, authentic apostolicity stands strong. It guards and defends the truth, disciplines the flawed, and emphasizes, affirms, and proclaims sound doctrine

Entrepreneurship and Creative Endeavor

Bringing new things into existence is also a means of making advancement into the darkness. Apostolic workers are frequently creative, on the edge, eager to try fresh things, willing to brave dangers, fearless, and entrepreneurial. They take risks and challenge the status quo. The Early Church turned their world upside down, and centuries later, we still need risk takers, adventurers, and creative thinkers who stand for God in the midst of a shifting culture. God chooses to use out-of-the-box thinkers and those who pursue innovative ministry endeavors not yet known to the structure. He is the author of creativity, and if we are listening to the Lord, we can be assured such ideas will be forthcoming.

We need risk takers, adventurers, and creative thinkers.

Still, these unusual ideas are sometimes not readily embraced in a Church culture more inclined to comfort. The struggle to follow God's vision and new approaches may bring conflict and challenge, perhaps even persecution. At times, conflict may be well-founded if the novel paradigms arise from human pride and challenge scriptural foundation. Those problems can fuel ongoing debates. In the midst of discussion, spiritual discernment is critically important so unusual ideas which are from God are not shut down while, on the other hand, human endeavors that are ill-advised or anti-scriptural do not move forward.

Once I (Carolyn) sat in Argentina with a U.S. mission team visiting with a major leader in one of the waves of the Argentine revival. Assemblies of God pastor Alberto Scataglini from La Plata told of sensing ahead of time that a special move of God was about to come, and he had been praying a great deal about it. A man came to visit him who was unknown to Alberto and most everyone at that time; he wanted to start an evangelistic crusade in the city. For various reasons he appeared at first to be an unlikely candidate to initiate this outreach. This young man told the elder leader about his conversion, subsequent Bible study and prayer, and his feeling that God wanted him to start reaching many people. He started to lay out a plan he felt the Lord had given him.

Pastor Scataglini said that as he talked, in his mind, he was nixing the ideas for various reasons. This inexperienced evangelist wanted to hold a big evangelistic outreach in a tent and within only a couple of weeks. Alberto felt no one would come to a tent (this had never been done in Argentina), and not in such a short period of time with little opportunity for spreading the word. Before the pastor opened his mouth, however, the Spirit said to him, "This man is from me, and I have sent him. I want you to do exactly what he wants."

Pastor Scataglini humbly said, "Okay. I am Elisha and you are Elijah. Tell me the details." Notice his discernment and his humble approach of saying he was the junior prophet. As a result, the church in La Plata became flooded with new converts. Miracles, wonders, and healings started immediately. Hundreds were made well, including some people whom the witch doctors had failed to heal. This so affected these occultic leaders that they converted, and if you went to one of the many witch doctor locations, it was not unusual to find a note on the door: "Closed. Gone to the crusade." Those who were demon possessed were set free, and the whole spiritual atmosphere shifted.

That young man was Carlos Annacondia who ultimately was used by God to bring hundreds of thousands of people to the Lord across Argentina and in many other countries around the world. This man is very humble, a family man, used greatly by God to push back the darkness in many places. But what would have happened if

Pastor Scataglini had not been sensitive and refused to support the "upstart's" unusual strategies?

As we think of Peter's and Paul's "new revelation" of incorporating Gentiles into the Early Church and the discussions held in Acts 11 and 15, discernment as to how the Spirit was leading proved absolutely essential. It was not the time to hold on to the old Jewish traditions. When the Pharisees and Sadducees had taken this approach with Jesus, they literally missed the Messiah when he was standing right in front of them.

Spirit-led insight is required to make decisions about all kinds of endeavors. Assuredly, God-ideas for apostolic functions require support, development, resourcing, and encouragement. True spiritual leaders are not overcome by the temporal but challenged to rise up and achieve the divine directive to which they are called.

Many leaders are transitioning into authentic apostolic ministry across the global Church, and it is a critical shift that needs to take place for the Church to advance in this day of ever-changing cultures. Amidst the fluctuations of society, God will provide calling and anointing for the workers required to implement His creative tactics. The Church needs people who are initiative-engaged, entrepreneurial, and fresh in their approaches.

The Church must move when and where God wants it.

Those in apostolic roles are anointed as change agents. They are the creative imaginary, the "what if?" person. They might be described as a mover and shaker. There are also other people who want to leave things as they are; they seem quite averse to change. Innovation might frighten them. But if the Church does not move when and where God wants it, then she will miss being prepared for His designed future.

The legendary hockey player, Wayne Gretzky, is known for saying, "I skate to where the puck is going to be, not to where it has been." If a church desires to "hang out" around where the puck has been, they will miss many opportunities. Only the Holy Spirit knows where the puck is going to be, and He wants us to skate there and be ready for what He has for us to do. Those functioning in the apostolic and the prophetic must hear from God, and then they will head "out there" where the puck is yet to be. Unfortunately, the Church has seemed to be reacting and playing catch up rather than meeting and greeting society when it arrives at the next spot. Imagine what that kind of influence would look like! The Holy Spirit can steer us there.

Apostolicity has the gift of leading out change and bringing expansion. Sometimes this can bring jealousy from those accustomed to dealing with the norm, but it need not if we come to understand and appreciate our different giftings and callings within the church. Jesus Himself was apostolic (along with the other four gifts), and He always seemed to be rocking the proverbial boat. Unfortunately, this caused jealous reactions from the temple leaders, escalating to such a point that they wanted to eliminate Him. Clearly, apostolicity helped take Jesus to the Cross. If only the Jews had recognized the real work of God in their midst!

As we experience innovative approaches, fresh direction, and unusual ideas, we desperately need discernment from the Lord—insight on when something should not be supported, but the courage to back God's plan. It often requires a hearty dose of fortitude and resolve to encourage entrepreneurial individuals to follow their godly visions, and to do this without a trace of jealousy or fear, trusting in the Lord to lead the way. God help us if we stifle someone God has called or take the wind out of their sails, discouraging or barring one of God's sent ones from accomplishing a daring task.

Flexibility and Moving From Place To Place

Those in apostolic roles not only lead change for the church, they also tend to need personal change. They have a drive, a calling, an urgency, to take the gospel to unreached places. Their desire is to see the Church established to the edge of the world, and somehow, they cannot stay still. Once new territory has been cleared, the foundation is set, and the church is strong with a developed team of local leaders, then apostolic leaders become restless and are ready to move on.

Any work established apostolically needs to understand the Spirit will ultimately send their founder to another place. Unfortunately, apostolic leaders sometimes wander from their callings, drifting into other five-fold gifts and stagnating in a comfortable place. However, churches with leaders who continue the pursuit of growing, planting, and reaching into yet another uncharted territory will need to comprehend when God is calling the person on. Those functioning in the apostolic will complete the assignment God sent them to accomplish and then move ahead to the next project someplace else, doing this again and again. Be ready to pray for them and send them off, but keep in contact. You will need one another in the days and years ahead.

There is no competition among God-called five-fold leaders.

It is apparent the New Testament apostles were generally respected by the churches which they had founded, since local church teams often went back to them for advice. This is as it should be. There is no competition among God-called five-fold leaders. The previous apostolic work should be honored by those who are presently building upon it. Those who are there now should prayerfully strive to avoid resistance, jealousy, dishonor, divisiveness, the tearing down of the past ministries, or the evading of prior leaders. They should acknowledge God's divine seasons and plans in both their present work and that of the past. Those first leaders paid a price to clear the way and establish the church in that place. Good leaders remember those who paved the way.

I (Joe) am aware of a situation where a pastor faced a most difficult challenge. The pastor had left a long-term pastorate of a successfully missions-oriented church where there had been a mutual love and appreciation for and from the entire church family. Years of doing life and ministry day in and out, with a long-term multi-staff, led to the development of wonderful and enriching relationships. While it was well understood and respected that the pastor should cleanly leave the congregation and allow the new pastor to take the helm, the transition had led this pastor to a role that was no longer pastoring a local congregation. It was a unique and positive transition.

Six months after leaving that pastorate however, the Christmas season had arrived and ended, and oddly, not one card or Christmas/New Year's greeting from the church's staff came his way. Somewhat confused, the pastor couldn't help but take it personally. For the life of him, he could not figure out what had gone wrong or why it appeared his closest friends for years had seemingly forgotten him and his young family.

Finally, a year or more later and almost accidentally, he heard from a church staff member that it had been—at the very least—hinted to the entire staff if they as much as sent a card to their former pastor they would be severely reprimanded. The former pastor had no desire to verify the truth of this statement, but it appeared to make sense. The pastor who had fulfilled the role after him admittedly had a strong business acumen, yet if the staff member was correct, it appeared he had little regard for Kingdom relationships that reach farther and longer than the local church. This new pastor, apparently trying to show himself strongly as an apostolic leader, had seemingly become demanding and dogmatic to his new staff in his attempt to take ownership of his new role and title. As much as this new pastor was possibly presenting himself as his own version of an apostolic and innovative leader, if these things were correct, he missed the mark.

Pastors who leave ministries do well to respectfully show ministerial courtesy and not involve themselves unduly with the new pastor's ministries or the congregation. Similarly, it behooves newly arriving pastors to honor the past when at all possible for the sake of building unified strength for further apostolic growth in reaching the lost and building God's Kingdom.

When communication is kept open between the ones who originally established the church and new leaders who are coming in, many positive results can occur. We see from the New Testament apostles that they had a logical interest in how the churches were proceeding. After all, they had laid the groundwork and paid a price to set the foundation, so they naturally continued to have a concern for the health and welfare of those former churches. The new pastors communicated with their apostolic founder and asked them to provide wisdom, help settle disputes, correct doctrine, maintain church unity, and other ongoing connections. Observe that the New Testament apostles founded the churches to which they were connected and did not set themselves over those churches or ask unknown churches to come under their supervision.

It should also be noted that Paul often talked about his "laboring" so as not to be a burden to anyone. Apostolic leaders must be prepared to leave when they are called—to be free to move on and not feel bound to a salary or place. As a tentmaker, Paul was not out money-grubbing from anybody. He expected no offerings, though he received some. But Paul remained active at his tentmaking, while being an apostolic church planter. This meant he made other connections in society. It also allowed him to move easily from place to place—to pick up and go when the Spirit prompted, thereby expanding his influence and relationship base.

Chapter Four

Apostolicity and Relationships

*"By thy reconciling love
every stumbling block remove;
each to each unite, endear;
come, and spread thy banner here."*[27]
Charles Wesley

The final set of themes regarding apostolic functions all have to do with relationships. In order to accomplish apostolic tasks, others are needed to help. Team work is critical. Humbly leading by example and influence is vital to apostolicity. A key is to seek the Lord for insight, wisdom, and the right words to share in sticky situations.

Maintaining unity

The Early Church was riddled with problems. It was not an idyllic, conflict-free zone. Wherever we have humanity, we will have clashes. The apostles clearly saw it as their responsibility to confront and manage this conflict and do everything they could to help maintain church unity. They gave instruction regarding lawsuits among believers (1 Cor. 6:1-11), addressed factions (1 Cor. 4), and provided numerous exhortations about living in harmony.

When church members did not get along, the apostles "fought" for unity: "I plead with Euodia and I plead with Syntyche to be of the same mind in the Lord. Yes, and I ask you, my true companion, help these women..." (Phil. 4:2-3). Apostolicity has the tasks of challenging people to unify and assisting in conflict management.

Van Yperen says genuine reconciliation, which is the goal of conflict management, "assumes and requires submission in three ways: to God, to one another, and to authority."[28] He further states, "Most church conflict is about submission, not obedience. Without submission, there is no church."[29] Should apostolic workers themselves choose not to model submission to authority in their own lives, they do nothing to bring the church to maturity and often cause further damage to the church at large.

Philippians 2:3 provides this challenge: "Do nothing out of selfish ambition or vain conceit, but in humility consider others better than yourselves." Carrying this out in real life requires an inbred core devoid of pretention and arrogance. It does not allow for posturing or a show of self-importance. When those kinds of selfish traits are present, problems and contentions naturally arise.

In places where the early churches were established, the apostles faced the necessity of dealing with their ongoing troubles. The apostles would begin a church and move on, but they still kept contact with those churches and helped resolve problems, handling a goodly number of controversies, people problems, schisms, disputes, irregularities, and other difficulties. This wasn't a "fun" authoritarian job full of personal ease and glory. It was and still is a weighty mantle requiring divine wisdom and anointing. Paul's letters and visits obviously attempted to assist in these various complications.

God uses apostolic workers to be an independent and unbiased help in times of conflict. These leaders are certainly gifts to the church. Paul noted, "Besides everything else, I face the daily pressure of my concerns for all the churches" (2 Cor. 11:28). Truly, the calling as ascribed is a weight, but those anointed for apostolicity are prepared by God to carry and embrace it. He provides sagacity, strength, courage, and insight as they follow Him.

The apostolic leader strives to recognize a path of reconciliation even in the most difficult situations. In their book *The Externally Focused Church*, Rick Rusaw and Eric Swanson offer, "Reconciliation can happen even when resolution does not."[30] Opposition, disagreement, resistance, and conflict results in varied categories of suffering for apostolic leadership. The table below highlights some of the common conflict management matters

Apostolicity and Relationships

regularly addressed by leaders, most of which were common to the Early Church apostles.

Common Conflict Management Encounters for Church Leaders

- Communication Mishaps
- Delivering Bad News
- Opening Closed Minds
- Handling Unfair Criticism
- Crisis Communication
- Firing Staff
- Removing a Pastor from His or Her Church
- Dealing with Unreasonable Requests
- Building Relationships Between Pastor/Board/Staff
- Perceptions and Misperceptions
- Handling Media During a Crisis
- Specially Called Meetings/Business Meetings
- Handling Complaints from Parishioners about Clergy
- The Fear of Failure
- The Fear of Freshness; Saying Something New
- The Attempt of Rebranding Culture
- Applying Spiritual Process to the Carnally Minded
- The Challenge of Not Becoming Cynical
- Loneliness
- Disagreeing or Changing Decisions of a Predecessor
- Financial and Budgetary Concerns
- Engaging Uninvolved Pastors and Churches in the Cooperative Fellowship
- The Challenge of Church Planting
- The Challenge of Church Revitalization
- Balancing Personal Life with Scheduling Demands
- The Challenge of Developing Departmental Ministries at a State/District Level

- Balancing Act: Taking Time for Personal Scripture Study and Prayer
- Handling Litigation and Lawsuits
- Betrayal by a Trusted Friend or Confidant
- Encountering Immoral and/or Unethical Ministers

Apostolic leaders should always find the point of reconciliation.

Scripture has many guidelines regarding conflict. Second Timothy 2:24 says, "And the Lord's servant must not quarrel; instead, he must be kind to everyone, able to teach, not resentful." Additionally, Colossians 3:13 states, "Bear with each other and forgive whatever grievances you may have against one another. Forgive as the Lord forgave you."

Of all the topics for apostolic discussion, biblical truth is the foremost of a church leader's considerations and must be used during reconciliation activities. Conflict is a broken relationship. The goal of apostolic leaders should always be to find the point of reconciliation with the Bible as his or her guide. They should aim to honor God, cultivate wholesomeness, preserve the well-being of the ministry, and accomplish necessary repentance and restoration in managing matters of conflict and doctrinal differences.

While reconciliation and restoration are the aims, there remains an apostolic duty and responsibility to address matters adversely impacting God's Kingdom. Clarence St. John, former Assemblies of God superintendent of the Minnesota District, said, "The Lord told me that I would have to answer for those pastors who kill the churches and the board members who drive the churches to the ground. We have a responsibility to clean up those who are infecting and affecting the Church, [even though we] lose a friend or two along the way."[31]

We must always remember that conflict is a battle of spiritual warfare, both relational and spiritual in nature. Paul writes in Ephesians 6:12, "Our struggle is not against flesh and blood, but against the rulers, against the authorities, against the powers of this dark world and against the spiritual forces of evil in the heavenly realms." Van Yperen's words resonate powerfully: "Conflict is usually the result of many suns going down on unresolved and unreconciled issues. As time passes and sins go unconfessed, the many footholds can make a stronghold."[32] Conflict is a spiritual battle. Apostolicity partners with God to pull down those strongholds and establish the Church.

Knowing the basics of conflict management is a great asset for apostolic leaders. Scripture admonishes the shepherd to speak the truth in love (Eph. 4:15), while letting your "yes" be a plain "yes" and your "no" be a plain "no" (Matt. 5:37). Acting in humility, thinking more of others than one's self, and seeing things from other people's perspectives are important tasks for the shepherd-leader (Phil. 2:3-4). Always, one's work should be given to a voice seasoned with grace (Col. 4:6).

Church Discipline

Spirit-empowered leaders should be committed to furthering holiness in all situations. They must be willing to rebuke and discipline those who are harming the people of God and distorting God's truth. Galatians 6:1 tells how discipline should be carried out: "Brothers and sisters, if someone is caught in a sin, you who live by the Spirit should restore that person gently. But watch yourselves, or you also may be tempted." The one initiating the discipline must evidence spiritual maturity, divine wisdom, godly character, extreme care, and direction by the Holy Spirit. Apostolic leaders often have to take care of difficult situations where a person is caught in a sin, but this should be handled carefully and lovingly, all the while striving to lead the person to repentance and restoration.

Discipline within the church is designed specifically for believers involved in overt sin. Scripture puts emphasis upon Christians engaged in sexual immorality, people spreading false teachings, those creating discord or strife in the church body, and believers in outspoken rebellion to the spiritual authorities appointed by God. Indeed, it is important for the church to discipline itself (1 Cor. 5:12-13). Pastors and other local church leaders should correct their own people, and overseers or denominational leaders should discipline pastors if needed. No one is above a call to repentance. If church leaders ignore blatant sinfulness within the body of Christ, then they fail to honor the Lord's demand for the church to be holy (I Pet. 1:16), and this provides a bad testimony to the unchurched.

This apostolic labor, while not to be avoided, should also be administered prayerfully, graciously, yet firmly in light of God's sanctity.

Many leaders, attempting to follow what they interpret as scriptural process, misappropriate the matter and inadvertently cause more harm than healing. Pastors should learn not to administer discipline in a main service with all the church's visitors present. A great principle is that "the circle of confession" should only be as large as the "circle of offense." Presenting offenses to innocent congregants opens confusion and concerns which are not their burden to carry. Eager to deal with conflict, well-meaning elders or spiritual leaders often forget the whole idea of discipline is restoration. The church's leaders are to help bring healing rather than devastation. All confrontation must therefore be carried out with gentleness, love, and humility, seeking to restore the fallen brother or sister.

The aim is to help the individual while simultaneously maintaining the purity of the body of Christ. Discipline in the church should never be entered into lightly or for minor offenses. It is meant to be helpful, removing the sin that will ultimately create spiritual death and separation from God and others.

Hebrews 12 tells us that just as earthly fathers discipline their children for their good, so does God. "For the Lord disciplines the one he loves, and chastises every son whom he receives" (Heb. 12:6). Once the desired result of repentance has been realized, then the church must extend forgiveness, comfort, acceptance, and restoration to the individual (2 Cor. 2:5-8). An apostolic task is to oversee this whole process as redemptively as possible.

Team Building, Networking, and Resourcing

Those in apostolic roles are adept at creating links and forging connections that create synergy. They locate resources, persuade people to support the vision, and find mature disciples with the right talents and giftings to build their team. Often crossing denominational lines, they unify people to accomplish what they could never do by themselves. Apostolicity brings diverse kinds of people together, various ethnic groups, those from different countries, and assorted organizations. This cooperation brings the energy and fresh ideas that accomplish so much.

Acts 6:1-6 addresses the continuity of apostolicity through the elements of harmonious teamwork. Seeing Greek Jewish widows being overlooked by the Hebraic Jews during the distribution of food, the twelve apostles decided to build their team by adding seven people "full of the Spirit and wisdom" who could oversee the meals. This would allow them to focus their efforts on prayer and the ministry of the word. The apostles were happy with the choices made by the people, prayed, and laid hands on them.

This indicates that any sort of church leadership tasks requires those who are "full of the Spirit and wisdom." In this case, these leaders helped to head off a rising disagreement. Note also that the apostles' proposal of adding to the team "pleased the whole group," and the church people themselves made the choices which in turn were ratified by the apostles and the laying on of hands. Team building is a group matter, and careful attention needs to be given to the character, integrity, and faith of those selected.

Jesus also knew the importance of team selection and team building. In Luke 6:12-13 we learn that Jesus went to a mountainside and spent the night praying. "When morning came, he called his disciples to him and chose twelve of them, whom he also designated apostles." Jesus sought God regarding the selection of His team. Furthermore, he was clear about what he wanted them to do as shown in Luke 9:1-6: "When Jesus had called the Twelve together, he gave them power and authority to drive out all demons and to cure diseases, and he sent them out to proclaim the kingdom of God and to heal the sick." He continued with detailed instructions on how to proceed with this assignment. In Luke 10:1-24 He acts similarly in sending out the 72 two-by-two. He begins with appointing them to a particular mission task and explaining the purpose and procedures to follow. At the end of this passage He provides more instruction to his Twelve.

Clearly Jesus was thoughtfully training different sized groups. He chose His instructions, explanations, and experiences carefully for each grouping. With His twelve disciples, He was always spending additional time with them, taking them aside privately, further unfolding God's plan, and giving deeper, more complex insights into the Kingdom of God. He was fitting the discipleship experiences to individualized levels of maturity and preparing them for differing future assignments after He was gone.

Jesus was a mentor par excellence. Barnabas followed Jesus' example in this. He stood by Paul when the Damascus Road dust was barely off his feet, taking him to the apostles and vouching for him after his conversion. Several years later Barnabas looked up Paul who had seemingly been overlooked and forgotten by the established Church. He took Paul to Antioch, staying by him while he built trusted relationships and became a respected teacher. As we have seen, it is Paul and Barnabas who are then chosen by the Antioch church and sent out as apostles among the Gentiles. Barnabas accompanies Paul on his first missionary journey, taking on Mark at the end of the journey as his new mentee, while Paul leaves with Silas.

Another related apostolic function is to discern in the Spirit the calling and potential of others. Apostolic workers are involved in selecting leaders to fulfill ministries so they can move on to their next apostolic post. They also sense from the Spirit who should be sent and where. Training and mentoring ensue, geared toward demonstrating and teaching how to function in apostolic or other leadership roles. In short, apostolicity recognizes and trains up more people with an apostolic heart. Paul not only went himself but sent off Timothy and Erastus to Macedonia (Acts 19:22), stationed Timothy in Ephesus, (1 Tim. 1:3), and assigned Titus to Crete (Titus 1:5). From his letters to Timothy, we clearly see Paul training and mentoring him and building Timothy up in his calling. Learning comes from doing life and ministry together.

We become like the persons with whom we spend the most time. Roderick Evans writes, "The apostle will love the Church as a father loves his children. His personality in the Church will resemble that of a father. Apostles mentored and developed "sons" in the faith: "I am not writing this to shame you, but to warn you, as my dear children. Even though you have ten thousand guardians in Christ, you do not have many fathers, for in Christ Jesus I became your father through the gospel" (1 Cor. 4:14-15). Perhaps one of the clearest functions of apostolic leadership is that they serve as spiritual parents in fostering and developing new leaders. For them, this is a very conscious task—one that takes time and thought.

The New Testament apostles commissioned and ordained people called by the Spirit to various ministries (1 Tim. 4:14; 2 Tim. 1:6-7; Acts 6:6). Astute discernment is required to see in those under one's care what they may not see in themselves. Training and cultivating next-generational leadership characterize apostolic leadership at its core since this strengthens the foundation of the on-going Church.

Another crucial role of apostolicity is connecting the churches and networking people. Since they were endlessly traveling, the apostles often carried letters from place to place, brought news of how the various churches were doing, and led congregations into prayer for other churches and territories. Like building teams of people, networks of churches—often across denominational lines—can accomplish more and shine a spotlight on new ministries. We are stronger together! I (Joe) recently called the national bishop of a different denomination to discuss statements of ecumenical agreement. It was joyous to pray together, recognizing Kingdom strategies are strengthened when leaders across the body of Christ work in unity.

The early apostles were also resource developers, both in people and in funds. They often sent emissaries out to accomplish networking tasks. In Philippians, 1 Thessalonians, and 1 Corinthians, Paul mentions sending off leaders such as Timothy, Epaphroditus, and others. It is said Paul started fourteen churches and some believe it may be as high as twenty[33] with many more begun by his ministry apprentices. This allowed fresh input and giftings to be spread abroad.

The early apostles were networkers and resource developers.

The apostles received offerings from the Gentiles to help with needs, particularly for the poor in Jerusalem. Paul's letters have a number of references to offerings including 1 Corinthians 16:1-4, 2 Corinthians 8:1-9, and Romans 15:14-32. Clearly Paul saw these tasks as part of his apostolic calling.

We should too. God is calling men and women to apostolic ministry and we, the Church, are not stewarding that call very well. We need to treasure those He is calling, and we have the responsibility to strengthen and enable His call on their lives and to help resource their dreams and needs.

Inclusivity and Cultural Contextualization

The apostles moved among different cultural situations, being particularly adept at contextualizing the gospel. The church was not established in the old Jewish form, of course, but rather innovative approaches were developed that fit each culture. The church leadership was local and indigenous, and the church was self-governing, self-sustaining, and self-propagating. Each church had the opportunity to translate the Truth into its own context.

In Peter's culinary vision of various animals (Acts 10:9-16), the sheet or sail was let down by four corners, suggesting the four corners of the world. Given his reaction to being told to eat, there were unclean animals but perhaps also clean animals. The InterVarsity commentary states, "The vision's purpose—proving a new freedom in association of Jew and Gentile—is best accomplished if a mixture is present."[34] With Peter's subsequent visit to Cornelius who also had a vision, the idea of the Jews being the only ones God worked through was thrown to the wind. God had baptized the Gentiles in the Spirit, and the gift of speaking in tongues made that perfectly clear. No one could successfully argue that God wanted His church to be diverse and for fresh associations to begin.

When it comes to Jesus Himself, He stated that He was called to Israel. Nonetheless, He spoke to a Samaritan woman at the well and ministered in her town of Sychar (John 4:4-42). He healed/set free from a demon the child of a Syro-Phoenician woman (Mark 7:25-30) because He saw her faith. Jesus' parable of the Good Samaritan pits the mercy of someone from the despised group of Samaritans against the lack of compassion evidenced by a Levite and a priest, choosing the non-Jew to be the "neighborly" one. Then He clearly gives final instructions to the Eleven to "make disciples of all nations" (Matt. 28:19).

God wanted a house of prayer for all the nations.

Even the Temple had a place for the Gentiles when they visited there. It was the outer court, and there was a dividing wall with a sign proclaiming that the Gentiles (even as converted Jews) could not come into the inner court. T.W. Manson offered some interesting insight about this at a lecture in London in 1954. He discussed Mark 11:15-17 where Jesus cleansed the Temple and drove out the sellers. Here Jesus quoted a verse from Isaiah 56:7 stating, "My house will be called a house of prayer for *all the nations*" (emphasis the authors').

We usually have thought of these verses as a financial matter, stating that Jesus didn't like the buying and selling. Manson, however, believes that Jesus was really upset, not just with the sellers, but specifically with the fact that they were occupying the outer courts, the only place where the Gentiles could come and pray.[35] The Gentiles were being pushed out of their space! People were coming and going, hawking and dragging animals in and out. How could a person pray in such an atmosphere? In Mark, Jesus pointed out that the Temple was a house of prayer for everybody, even the Gentiles—all the nations. He did not want them shut out from the opportunity to seek God. It was more of a racial issue, a lack of extending sensitivity cross-culturally. The Gentiles would soon be welcomed into the Church, and Jesus started early to insist upon it, evidencing the most anger we ever see from Him.

Manson ended his lecture by stating that Jesus spent most of His time with the Jews because He was wanting to establish a leadership that was ready, after He departed, to include all people in His new Church:

> [Jesus was] building up within Israel a body of men and women who were set free from chauvinistic nationalism, from the ambition to impose Israelite ideals of faith and conduct on the rest of the world by force of arms; men and women set free from spiritual pride with its condescending readiness to instruct lesser breeds in the elements of true religion and sound morality; men and women who had learned in apprenticeship to Jesus how to accept the rule of God for themselves, and how to extend it to their neighbours at home and abroad by serving them in love. I think that Jesus saw the immediate task as that of creating such a community within Israel, in the faith that it would transform the life of his own people, and that a transformed Israel would transform the world.[36]

On the day of Pentecost, we see the apostles speaking in tongues so all the Gentile believers who were in town for the Feast of Pentecost (Shavuot) could hear the gospel message in their own language. As the Church gradually awakened to its full mission of being a blessing to all nations, it was certainly a revolutionary idea! Think of the shifts in perspective necessary for zealous, Jewish Paul to come to the place of making this statement in Galatians 3:28: "There is neither Jew nor Gentile, neither slave nor free, nor is there male and female, for you are all one in Christ Jesus." This attitude would have shaken up the world at that time, and it still does today.

On the first night of Hanukkah, 2018, anti-Semitism left Pittsburgh, Pennsylvania in grief with senseless murders of Jewish worshipers at Tree of Life Synagogue. On a visit to the city only weeks afterward, I (Joe) purposely drove by the location, witnessing the make-shift memorial of flowers and candles still in sight on the synagogue lawn. Racist challenges remain as a plague to our world today. Nonetheless, apostolic leaders must still widely and unambiguously espouse the truth of the gospel being for all people—every single one.

The modern-day church leader yet contends with cultural challenges for the appointment and deployment of God-called women in ministry. Junia(s) was at least one woman with apostolic calling in the New Testament, as declared by the apostle Paul (Rom. 16:7). It is the apostolic leader who will break barriers of sexism and forge new territories for women in ministry, taking the work of the Church in a relevant fashion to a shifting culture through apostolic reform.[37] David Cartledge noted, "It is inconceivable that a woman is to receive the same anointing as a man, and then be limited in expressing this."[38]

Anointed apostles will not be sexist, racist, cater to the rich, or show cultural disdain.

In my (Joe's) doctoral dissertation, I stated: "The call of God and the enabling of the Holy Spirit is not gender specific. A woman may have equal or more-so leadership and ministry as a male counterpart. Today's postmodern age deals with this same age-old dilemma of the authority and leadership of women in ministry. The Church continues to battle over the usage and placement of women. The undeniable key is whether or not an elected official or superintendent is willing to embrace the calling and pursue the ministry of apostolicity."[39]

Indeed, anointed apostles will not be sexist, play favoritism, cater to the rich or neglect the poor, be racist or intolerant, show cultural disdain, or participate in any factors that create unfairness or injustice. Jesus was careful not to think or behave in this way, and so the ones He chooses to send as His emissaries may not either.

Apostolic leaders who move into unreached territory and deal with various people groups must function without pride, arrogance, or subtle ideas of superiority. They may not demean others. They need to be culturally sensitive and ask God for the wisdom to contextualize the gospel without negative aspects of syncretism. Apostolic leaders cannot impose control and insist on their own ways, but rather they should humbly come alongside to support the building and growth of the indigenous church.

Apostolicity continues Jesus' work of tearing down the barrier of the dividing wall (consider the Temple and Eph. 2:14) so all people can come near to God. They maintain Jesus' emphasis on bringing justice and supporting others rather than stepping on them: "A bruised reed he will not break, and a smoldering wick he will not snuff out. In faithfulness he will bring forth justice" (Isa. 42:3). Just as the first apostles worked toward integrating the Jewish believers and the Gentile Christians, apostolicity today brings the same need for conscious efforts to unify.

Remember the Ephesians 4:12-13 verse which states that the purpose of the five gifts—including prophets and apostles—is "to equip his people for works of service, so that the body of Christ may be built up until we all reach unity in the faith and in the knowledge of the Son of God and become mature, attaining to the whole measure of the fullness of Christ" (emphasis the authors'). Notice the equipping is supposed to continue until we "all" reach unity in the faith. This is not an optional result; it is the consequence of the fivefold ministry doing their jobs, and it is right up there with knowing Jesus and becoming like Him. Real unity is actually a sign that we have attained to the fullness of Christ.

Apostolicity takes the lead in modeling and securing a Church that is open to all people. As hard as the challenge must have been to assimilate both Jews and Gentiles into a unified Church, this is exactly what the apostles did. As Jesus angrily cleared the Outer Courts so the Gentiles could pray, so, too, apostolic leaders will go to any lengths to sweep away what hinders people from the gospel and keeps them from fulfilling God's call on their lives.

Attitudes for Apostolicity

In dealing with others, the core of effective interaction and ministry is found in the heart and disposition of apostolic leaders themselves. Apostolic function must not exude an overwhelming, controlling, manipulative, or domineering attitude. For the apostolic leader, there is a fine component of stewarding one's authority sacredly, according to Doug Clay, general superintendent of the Assemblies of God.[40]

Apostolic leaders are God's representatives to His people. They are the shepherds of God's flock—not the shearer of the sheep, but the feeder of the sheep. They are to lead the flock to greener pastures (Ps. 23) and still or calm waters, not raging or dangerous rapids. These leaders carry heavy responsibilities: training and maturing believers, preaching and teaching, countering false teachings, being an example in word and in deed, conduct, love, spirit, faith and purity (1 Tim. 4:12). The work of the shepherd is not accomplished through personal accolades or talent but by the Spirit of God.

The apostolic minister should always follow the pattern of Paul's words to the Ephesians in chapters 4, 5, and 6. Walk in unity (Eph. 4:1-3). Walk in purity (4:17-19). Walk in love (5:1-2). Walk in light (5:8-11). Walk carefully (5:15-17). Walk in harmony with your spouse (5:22-27). Walk in power (6:10-20). These attributes will encourage the leader to keep the initial excitement of the calling passionately active in their lives while weakening the discouragements that easily come with the challenges.

We need more people of towels and humility.

Jesus addressed His own leadership attitude as that of a servant. The study of apostolic ministry needs to include the life and ministry of Christ in order to be fully orbed. In Mark 10:43-44, Jesus says, "Whoever wants to become great among you must be your servant, and whoever wants to be first must be slave of all." Today's Church needs more people of towels and humility and fewer people scurrying for their seat at the head table. We are not supposed to be producing celebrities. Luke 14:7-11 speaks of leaders humbling themselves and waiting for God, the sender, to exalt them. Mark 10:32-40 defines leaders as followers of Christ rather than those who seek positions of prestige. Servant leadership is not about position or authority. Apostolic leadership is that of both strength and humility, dedicated to the calling rather than title or position.

A memorable legend tells of the day in A.D. 371 that St. Martin of Tours was made a bishop —a position requiring apostolic function just like other bishops, superintendents, and denominational leaders today. They came after him, but he did not want the job and hid in a haystack in a barn. It was full of geese who gave his position away, but Martin's attitude is excellent. Anybody who is proud enough to desire a position such as this should not receive it.

Mark 10:41-45 addresses servant leaders as those who give up personal rights to develop the greatness in others. Jesus' approach to servant leadership acknowledges full trust in God alone. The risk of serving others is strengthened by the knowledge that God is in control of all things, whatsoever may come to pass. With the example of Jesus washing the disciples' feet in John 13:4-11, God-called leaders realize their hope in Christ by becoming servants. For an apostolic leader, this constitutes a direct example of the greatest test of leadership: That one may very well need to wash the feet of those who have, or will, cause harm and conflict. Jesus washed the feet of Judas.

Apostolicity is involved in ongoing foot washing in every circumstance.

In 2004 when elected as a denominational superintendent, I (Joe)—not fully recognizing then the impact of the role or symbolic nature of the act—tearfully and genuinely took a towel during the state-wide conference and knelt during a communion service to wipe the shoes/feet of each of the other presently-serving state leaders and that of the national General Superintendent, Dr. Thomas Trask. The very sign of doing it became symbolic of a spiritual commitment for the calling and mantle just received. Apostolicity is involved in ongoing foot washing in every circumstance.

Apostolicity may engage in many tasks such as nurturing the flock of God, defending the gospel, performing rites, managing the church, developing, ordaining, officiating, preaching and teaching, representing, coordinating, inaugurating, and executing faithfully the work of God. The multitude of daily tasks, however, should not overshadow the inward attitude of servanthood. Believers want to follow those who are themselves following Jesus; they care more about that than excellence of CEO style management. The "To Do List" cannot be allowed to push out the time needed to hear from God. Leaders must find the space to keep their own soul and spirit healthy and thriving through prayer, personal solitude, Bible reading, fasting, and other spiritual disciplines. It is critically important to maintain a living, vibrant relationship with God.

Worldly thinking regarding leadership gimmicks must be replaced with a saturation of God's Spirit.

When prayer is an attitude of the heart, the Lord will guide, reveal wisdom, give vision and direction, activate the spiritual gifts, and provide words at the very moment they are needed. Functioning well in the apostolic demands a lifestyle of being attached to the vine. The thinking of the world regarding leadership gimmicks must be replaced with a saturation of the Spirit of God. The Lord will then direct according to His heart, showing leaders where to go and how best to share the good news.

Church leaders should never allow personal agendas and busyness to skew their emphasis on reaching the lost. Even maturing the Church into Jesus' likeness has this as an ultimate end since He came "to seek and to save the lost" (Luke 19:10). The apostolic calling in the church must be retained as a primary focus.

Even some reading this book now may find yourselves moved by the Holy Spirit—as a prodigal son or daughter—to return to the good and faithful Savior (Luke 15:11-32) who awaits a humble and repentant heart. God is a loving Father who will run to meet you, place a robe on your back and a ring on your finger in celebration that His child, once considered dead, is now alive again. All you need to do is repent and call out to Him. He always hears a repentant heart. (See Romans 3:23, 6:23, 5:8, John 1:12, Ephesians 2:8-9, Revelation 3:20, Luke 24:46-48, Acts 3:19).

Eckhard Schnabel writes, "The goal of Paul's missionary work was the conversion of Jews and pagans to faith in Jesus Messiah, Savior and Lord, the transformation of traditional patterns of religious, ethical and social behavior, and the integration into the community of fellow believers."[41] Today's apostolic work continues with the primary task of reaching all types of people from all kinds of places who have not heard or accepted grace-given salvation through faith in Jesus Christ.

Apostolic gifts often flow with prophetic overtures. Let us now turn our attention to prophecy.

Chapter Five

The Prophetic Core

*"Earth's crammed with heaven,
And every common bush afire with God;
And only he who sees takes off his shoes.
The rest sit around it and pluck blackberries."*[42]
Elizabeth Barrett Browning

Prophecy energized the apostolic church. The prophetic helps bring the one and only uncommon God into the midst of common circumstances. In order to see God at work, however, we have to keep our eyes and ears open. Our spirits need to be sensitized to God's voice, His ways, and those holy moments occurring right in front of us. If we are too busy with our own activities, we will overlook the bush burning and miss God speaking. When he came over to inspect the burning bush, Moses actually had to be told by God to take off his sandals because the place was holy (Ex. 3:5). Moses was close to overlooking the sanctity and seriousness of the very moment about to change his whole life.

Since the prophetic consists of God communicating with us, we need individuals in the church who will spend time with the Lord and share what they have heard and seen. Likewise, we must have a church that is willing to listen carefully. Otherwise they might miss what He is saying and doing because they "sit around picking blackberries." (See poem above.)

What exactly is the prophetic and how does it properly function? How do we recognize it when it occurs? Since the prophetic functions informally and not just by stating, "Thus saith the Lord," we need to be spiritually aware so our hearts quicken when God speaks through whatever means He chooses. A prophecy should not be recognized by the fact that someone claims to speak for God. The claim itself does not make it so. False prophets can make such claims and confuse the church. Rather, listeners should recognize a genuine prophetic word may come naturally and without announcement. We all need hearts open to receive whatever is truly from God. Jesus often accompanied a truth from the Father by saying, "He who has ears to hear, let him hear."

> *We can be so busy with our own agendas and opinions that we don't hear God.*

Not only did Jesus talk about listening, but He also pointed out in multiple places that He spoke only the words the Father wanted Him to say. He did not, however, announce this each and every time. He simply spoke and expected his listeners to hear—then open their lives and let the word of God enter in. The parable of the sower recorded in Matthew 13 demonstrates the importance of this. God may be communicating to us through many different methods. We have to listen in a variety of situations because He can speak when we least expect it, just like when Moses experienced the burning bush in the midst of his every day work of tending the flocks. Sometimes we are so busy with what we want to say and with our own personal agendas and opinions that we aren't paying attention to the Lord.

We may open our ears when the Lord speaks in a church service, but if that is the only time we really listen, we are relegating God's on-going involvement to a very narrow segment of time. He wants to be so regularly involved in our lives that He designated the prophetic as one of the five most important functions of the church, alongside evangelism, pastoring, teaching, and the apostolic. For those skeptical, that reason alone proves prophetic communication is biblical and an expected part of our faith journey with God.

The prophetic should work throughout our lives in a regular and normal capacity. As with the apostolic, we have not forged out ample understanding of the prophetic flow within the Church. Jesus relegated it to be not only a gift of the Spirit but a full-orbed responsibility amongst the five-fold ministry functions of the church. Why did Jesus decide to raise the prophetic to prominence among the leadership team? Is it really as vital as a pastor?

What's In the Term?

In order to understand the prophetic responsibilities and benefits to the Church, studying the root words for "prophet" is helpful. The prophet's work has two parts: 1) to receive the divine message and 2) to deliver that message faithfully. Both of these aspects are shown in the three Hebrew terms for "prophet." The Hebrew words *chozeh* or *ro'eh* indicated the prophets' role of grasping God's message as it was revealed to them. These words are often translated as "seer," i.e., a person who sees what God wants to do or say. The most frequently used Hebrew word for prophet was *nabi*, and it describes prophets as they convey their message through speech or in writing or other forms.

Both roles are mentioned in 1 Samuel 9:9: "Formerly in Israel, if someone went to inquire of God, they would say, 'Come, let us go to the seer [*ro'eh*]' because the prophet [*nabi*] of today used to be called a seer [*ro'eh*]." The other Hebrew word, *chozeh*—which is derived from the same Hebrew root from which we get our word for vision—emphasizes that the prophet receives messages through divinely initiated visions. Each of these three Hebrew terms for "prophet" underscores that role as the human side of God's ongoing divine communication.

In the New Testament, the Greek word corresponding to the Old Testament *nabi* is *prophetes*, (transliterated in English to "prophet"). Its basic meaning is "to speak forth."

The Old Testament obviously has numerous prophets which would take another book to study in depth, though we will incorporate a few examples. It may be important to note that just as a woman was included in the Bible as an apostle, so were many prophetesses (*nabia*) listed in the Old Testament such as Miriam (Ex. 15:20), Huldah (2 Kgs. 22:14-20; 2 Chron. 34:22-28), Deborah (as a judge, she was both a prophetess and a leader of Israel— Judges 4:4), Isaiah's wife (Isaiah 8:3), and one false female prophet, Noadiah (Neh. 6:14).

The prophetic ministry continued into the New Testament as well. The first time in the New Testament Church a prophet appeared by name was Anna (Luke 2:36-38) who prophesied over the young

Jesus and continued to speak of him to everyone looking for the Messiah. While the Early Church was being established, there was a group of prophets who went from Jerusalem to Antioch, including Agabus (Acts 11:27–30). Antioch developed its own group of resident prophets that involved Barnabas, Simeon, Lucius, Manaen, and Paul (Acts 13:1). After the Jerusalem Council they chose two leaders/prophets, Judas and Silas, to take the news back, and these two used their prophetic gifting, saying "much to encourage and strengthen the brothers" (Acts 15:22,32). Following Paul's third missionary journey, he stayed at the house of Philip the evangelist who "had four unmarried daughters who prophesied" (Acts 21:9). Since the book of Revelation is prophecy, this would give John prophetic status (Rev. 1:3).

A great deal of teaching about prophecy is scattered throughout Paul's letters. A study of New Testament prophets indicates there were prophetic groups in these various places such as Corinth, Rome, Thessaloniki, and Ephesus.[43] They traveled on occasion from church to church, and both men and women were recognized as prophets. Some of the apostles functioned as prophets, and generally prophets were not appointed to ruling functions in the church such as elder or bishop. Still, they exercised strong influence, along with apostles and elders, in the development of church doctrine and practice. The New Testament prophets provided inspired words that squared with apostolic doctrine and Scripture. No provision was given for appointing prophets in succeeding generations as a part of the church leadership structure.[44]

The Prophetic Flow

Many purposes exist for the free flow of the prophetic in the Church. God's intention is for the prophetic to cleanse and correct. It allows for God's voice to be heard in the church so He can interact in our lives and provide direction for the Body of Christ. The Lord uses prophecy to warn, foretell, guide/direct, shift, change, enlighten, encourage, build up, exhort, assure, motivate, console, cleanse, confirm, and provide vision and courage. 1 Corinthians 14:3 says, "But the one who prophesies speaks to people for their strengthening, encouraging and comfort."

The prophetic serves as a spring of God's involvement in the Church today. If this goes leaderless or is neglected, however, then a myriad of problems can enter from godless sources. Just as church members can go astray without a pastor, people can go unsaved without an evangelist, new believers can stay immature without a teacher, and the church does not reach out without the apostolic, likewise the Church can go without direction, strengthening, and cleansing if it is missing the prophetic word of the Lord.

> *CEO-style leadership along with structure and programming has squeezed out the Spirit.*

The lack of prophetic flow in the Church has allowed for a proliferation of the designs, control, and direction of human will. Instead of a fresh and ongoing spring of interaction with God so He Himself can lead the Church, we have unfortunately trended toward believing we are capable of handling things quite well on our own. This has resulted in CEO-style leadership in churches satiated with structure and programming, squeezing out the full move of the Spirit of God. Too often if leaders find themselves in a pinch, then they will call on Him, but otherwise independent thought seems to serve quite nicely. God does not exist simply to bless the work we have dreamt up. He Himself longs to provide us with His own vision and to help us accomplish it His way—building on what He has done in the past, honoring His holy presence of the present, and recognizing the future only the Triune Godhead can direct.

Ephesians 4:11 states that Christ gave the five ministry roles to flow in the church. He Himself chose prophecy to place among the five. No human made up this level of importance; it is God's own plan. He apparently felt it was as important a leadership role in the Church as evangelism, pastoring, teaching, and apostolicity. As a matter of fact, prophecy is the only gift mentioned every single time there is a list of spiritual gifts in Scripture.

The prophetic should be more than an oral message spoken occasionally in a Sunday morning service. That is the operation of one of the gifts of the Spirit, but the pouring forth of this stream is meant to be more pervasive, robust, and applicable to numerous situations. The full work of the prophetic is designed to occur at many times throughout the week and to be an integral part of the life of the church. Any gathering of the Body of Christ for meetings, teaching, worship, or anything at all, really, is an opportunity for

God to be present to speak and guide.

When a person has a deep prayer life, has heard from God, and shares something in a meeting he or she believes is from the Lord, this is the prophetic in action. The prophetic does not have to occur formally but rather can happen naturally. Quite honestly, it was never intended to be odd or strange but a natural flow of God's relationship in our lives.

In fact, all of the five-fold ministry gifts and church leadership functions (Eph. 4:11) occur naturally and normally. A pastor does not step up and announce, "Thus saith the Lord, I am now going to pastor you." A teacher simply proceeds to teach, and an evangelist easily shares the good news. The prophetic can be delivered unpretentiously within a regular day, and the Lord has no limits to His creative venues for prophetic release.

The prophetic should issue forth freely and involve both sound leadership and various congregants. This inclusion of many in the body to serve in a particular function happens in each of the five-fold ministries in the Church. For example, numerous Christians witness and serve in evangelistic ministries, but there are those who are especially gifted to win many to Christ and to train, model, and oversee this area as leaders. Many church members reach out to the community around them, but not all are called to apostolicity as missionaries or roles such as overseers or superintendents. Various parishioners help care for the sheep but are not called into pastoral leadership. Others serve in different teaching roles but are not theologians or conference speakers. Likewise, some are used in the gift of prophecy on occasion but are not called to lead out the prophetic flow of the church in a steadier capacity.

To put it another way, all prophets who have ever existed prophesy, but not all who prophesy can consider themselves prophetic leaders/prophets. That is God's selection and calling, and His alone. Some believe the prophet's function has ceased, but there is no evidence of this in Scripture. Certainly, prophecy continues, and churches today see no cessation of the gifts of the Spirit nor of the five-fold ministry gifts. The Body of Christ still needs all God has provided for its vital functioning. May the prophetic gifts move as the Spirit provides, and may prophetic leadership arise who will humbly serve in this arena.

Hearing from God

Working in the prophetic is essentially a call to spend much time with God. The Lord will shape the person used in the prophetic, helping them to grow in the fear of the Lord, to recognize His Voice quickly, and to be willing to do and say whatever God desires no matter the consequences.

Unfortunately, some people do not really want to hear what God desires to say, especially if it is from somebody else in the Body of Christ. A few make comments such as "I don't need someone else telling me anything. I can hear God on my own." Why can't God speak to every person for Himself? Well, He can. After all, His sheep know His voice (John 10:1-5). However, some people choose not to spend the time to hear. Others are listening but are frightened to walk in the bold level of faith God expects; they need confirmation. The inner character and lifestyle of some are not inclined toward God, and their personal desires get in the way. Still others are in open rebellion against God and need help to return. An example of this was David when he was not facing his sin of taking Uriah's wife and then having Uriah killed. The prophet Nathan found and confronted him so David would repent and renew his relationship with God (2 Sam. 12).

In the midst of such instances, God desires to speak through a vessel which is as pure as possible and willing to deliver His own words. He is not looking for an abridged or purposefully softened approach. The Father wants to testify—which is to "serve as evidence or proof of something's existing or being the case."[45] God uses the prophetic to testify about what is accurate and true, about what the future holds, and about His view of our lives and circumstances. He might assess certain areas positively, commending or encouraging us, or He might feel some things are not acceptable for us to maintain or that the direction we are heading is incorrect. Through prophecy, God delivers His testimony, as He did through Nathan. And, yes, God does still speak in this very personal way to His followers today. But only "he who has ears" will hear.

In Revelation 19:9b-10 (NASB) John states something very important to the angel who was speaking to him:

> And he said to me, "These are true words of God." Then I fell at his feet to worship him. But he said to me, "Do not do that; I am a fellow

servant of yours and your brethren who hold the testimony of Jesus; worship God. For the testimony of Jesus is the spirit of prophecy".

What does this mean—the testimony of Jesus is the spirit of prophecy? Jesus is still alive and active so He continues to speak to us. Through prophecy Jesus testifies to what His Father continues to share with Him. All the way through the gospel of John, Jesus makes the point that He was speaking exactly what God wanted—sharing Truth from God Himself. He indicated that He and the Father were one. He knew His Father's voice and followed precisely what He wanted, not doing anything on His own initiative (John 8:28 NASB). If Christ is in us and we really wish to be like Him, we will seek to do the same. We will hear from Him and speak what He wants. Jesus is testifying to God's own words; this is the very spirit of prophecy itself.

False prophets are different. Jeremiah 23:16-18 refers to false prophets who speak on their own:

> This is what the Lord Almighty says, "Do not listen to what the prophets are prophesying to you; they will fill you with false hopes. They speak visions from their own minds, not from the mouth of the Lord. They keep saying to those who despise me, 'The Lord says: You will have peace.' And to all who follow the stubbornness of their own hearts they say, 'No harm will come to you.' But which of them has stood in the council of the Lord to see or to hear his word? Who has listened and heard his word?"

CEO-style leadership along with structure and programming has squeezed out the Spirit.

Prophetic individuals called by God will need to spend time in the His Council Room. They must hear from God. This is absolutely essential. The source of the word to be communicated cannot originate or flow from anywhere else except from being in God's presence. It should never come from the wise thinking or ruminations of mankind. Rather it issues forth when believers called to the prophetic task of taking time to be with God.

The Root of the Iceberg: Prayer and Intercession

Elmer L. Towns notes the importance of the intercessory role of a leader: "The heart of God is broken over the sin of His people, but more than that, the heart of God responds to the intercession of His servants."[46] Prayer makes a difference in the people who pray and in the situations for which they are interceding.

Those called to the prophetic will customarily be realized among the church's prayer warriors and intercessors. Their prayer life is similar to an iceberg: ninety percent under the water and ten percent out. The concealed life of anyone working in the prophetic is critical since the essence of the service entails listening to God and sharing His word when God releases it. Prayer provides the opportunity to know God and His voice, as opposed to personal thoughts and inclinations.

During this time hidden under the surface, prophetic servants are changed. They may be broken, become humbled, be convicted for their own part in the sin, and repent. Love for the people is poured out by the Lord so there is grief rather than haughtiness if correction is part of the message. Attitudes are cleared up, and their own ideas are removed. In short, they are prepared to be a clean vessel through whom God can properly work. These are matters today's Church leaders should consider when discerning God's words from prophetically inclined individuals.

When an individual receives a word from God, it does not necessarily follow that they should run out and share His plans and concerns immediately. Timing is of essence. The first task is to pray. Through this process, the Lord allows those called to the prophetic to gain clarity and perspective, deepening the message until they genuinely come to sense the heart of the Lord for that situation.

Often those called to the prophetic will be moved into intercession. In this kind of prayer, there is a gap standing between God and the individual, church, group, organization, state, or nation. One of the main roles of the prophetic is to grasp God's hand while simultaneously holding on to the situation. They must keep this posture until the two pull together. This can be so difficult because the intercessors don't want to let go of God nor do they want to let go of the situation. But the gap can be so large it becomes grueling.

Standing in the gap is often very ripping, strenuous, and difficult work. It may mean tears, cries of agony or moans, for a real intercessor doesn't just feel the pain in theory. Sometimes the prophetic message is never given because the one God spoke to has been faithful to intercede, and the Lord has changed the hearts and the circumstances. Things have cleared up without anything needing to be prophesied.

Those working in the prophetic also note where the breaks are in the wall of defense and then go to the gap and repair them (Ez. 13: 3-5). They are the watchmen on the wall who blow the trumpet to warn of an advancing enemy (Ex. 33: 1-11).

The church needs to know who these people are and appreciate their callings. *These intercessors are a defined element of the prophetic movement.* Often, they spend years sitting in church pews, unheard, unrecognized, with their gift unwelcomed. Like those being used in prophecy as a gift of the Spirit, not all intercessors are automatically prophetic leaders, but people with prophetic voices are almost certainly intercessors and can be found in the prayer ranks. Their labor will transform individuals and the church.

The work prophetic servants do in their "ninety percent under" status sometimes causes them to feel out of synch. As they are burdened and intercede for the changes God desires, they are often in a weeping stage while others are laughing. When others are enjoying their sin, prophetic servants are crying over it. However, when those who were once laughing ultimately repent and are crying at the altar, those operating in the prophetic are overjoyed and contented.

This can be more difficult than it seems. It's probably why prophets in the Old Testament wore sackcloth and sat in ashes. A scratchy cloth under clothes next to the skin can help a person bear with some rebellious, partying, ungodly, sinful matters in the world while the spirit is simultaneously being deeply grieved. That may be hard to understand in our contemporary society, but perhaps this is because we need more who are in synch with God's viewpoint instead of being in synch with the world's. While it may appear odd, I know people who have resorted to wearing burlap under their clothes in our modern times to try to bear up under a weight of intercession which the Lord has given them. Out of faithfulness in the prayer room, circumstances can shift.

Often prophetic servants are given a "holy discontent" from the Lord. This may be born in quiet for a time, but more often than not the Spirit ultimately wants to unveil that, using it to point out changes He desires to make. I suppose this could seem like a bad or critical attitude in the prophetic person (and if it's carnal, it is), but if the discontent is given by the Lord, others should hearken to it. During time spent in the iceberg root, God will prepare prophetic change-agents to speak forth a clarion appeal for modification or transformation. Then the Lord helps them deliver that message in the best way possible so it is most likely to be accepted.

A Call to Holiness

Sin separates us from God and our fellow human beings. One of the main purposes of prophetic function is to reconcile people back to God. The Lord desires His people to be holy and righteous, because in that state, they are most whole. When the clarion call of the prophetic voice is not heard in the Church, sin is often hidden, becomes more entrenched, and all the wages that sin exacts are collected.

A Pentecostal pioneer Melvin Hodges once said, "The New Testament Church gradually lost the purity and power that characterized her apostolic beginnings, and became adulterated by worldliness, greed and paganism as she increased in numbers and influence." He pondered whether the Pentecostal church would likewise stray from its biblical ideals and become corrupted by the world.⁴⁷ One of the main purposes of the prophetic is to put on the brakes.

When the Church fails to keep her prophetic message strong, moral decline occurs in society.

The prophetic call is not only needed for the Church but is also meant to be the moral conscience of society. It exposes and rebukes sin, offering the hope found in Jesus. The fact that our society is in moral decline makes us ponder why the Church failed to keep her prophetic message strong and clear. As the Church drifts morally and the prophetic is weakened, this in turn drastically affects society.

The prophetic is designed to carry out clean up detail. It seeks to tidy things up, scrub out the corners, wash down, prop up, put things in order, and disinfect, leaving everything sparkling clean and smelling with a sweet fragrance. The prophetic desires for this work of holiness to make the Church spotless, pure, and unencumbered in its service to the King. God uses His prophetic warnings and corrections to create clean hearts.

Before a housecleaning crew comes in, most people pick up clutter so surfaces are clear to dust off and the floors are free to be washed. Picking up is our part; cleaning up is God's part. We need to get rid of the mess in our lives and be willing to put things away or throw them out. When we are open to His work, the blood of Jesus will wash us, making us white as snow.

This kind of cleansing is not meant to be demeaning or cause shame. Rather it is designed to be a caring correction for our own good, seeking always to bring us back into right standing with God. This can actually be comforting, helping us know that the Father loves us enough to point out what needs to change. God doesn't want us pulled deeper into the clutches of sin.

The term "edification" does not mean "always positive."

Often people put emphasis on the edification part of the 1 Corinthians 14:3 (NASB) quote which says, "But the one who prophesies speaks to men for edification and exhortation and consolation." They use this to insist there should never be a negative or corrective prophecy. However, the term "edification" does not mean "always positive."

Something is edifying when it improves the mind or the character. We will be built up; we will get better by it. Certainly, we can be improved when we are reproved. Sometimes a word of correction is the most edifying of all. When the Father points out problem areas, He allows us to make changes and adjustments.

If we are doing something incorrectly, generally we would rather know it sooner (rather than later) so we don't fall into some bad habit. This applies to when we are learning to swim or ski or any other sport or skill, but it also pertains to our attitudes, lifestyles, and thinking. God cares enough to correct us and save us a lot of hassles. Even when He has to discipline us, this is good, because in actuality the correction is helpful toward our improvement.

Hebrews 12: 5-11 provides an important viewpoint on this:

And you have forgotten that word of encouragement that addresses

you as sons,

"My son, do not make light of the Lord's discipline, and do not lose heart when he rebukes you, because the Lord disciplines those he loves, and he punishes everyone he accepts as a son."

Endure hardship as discipline; God is treating you as sons. For what son is not disciplined by his father? If you are not disciplined (and everyone undergoes discipline), then you are illegitimate children and not true sons. Moreover, we have had human fathers who disciplined us and we respected them for it. How much more should we submit to the Father of our spirits and live! Our fathers disciplined us for a little while as they thought best; but God disciplines us for our good, that we may share his holiness. No discipline seems pleasant at the time, but painful. Later on, however, it produces a harvest of righteousness and peace for those who have been trained by it.

The prophetic can be used to share God's correction to us individually and as a church. If the plumb line is even a little off, we could build ourselves into the leaning tower of Pisa. The Lord wants the church to be built square and level, and so he uses this important work of His Spirit to take us into the future on a straight path. Actually, it is reassuring to know if we are needing it, we will get corrected. This is how we know we are adopted sons and daughters of the King and that He loves us enough to deal with us.

It is reassuring to know that if we need it, God will use the prophetic to correct us.

As with earthly fathers, sometimes the Lord might have to get stern so we become able to hear. The Lord starts softly and kindly. If we change, this may be all that is needed. But the message likely ramps up if we do not pay attention. Consider a father and his child. Dad may start a correcting process with a gentle reminder and a smile. However, after the twentieth attempt, the father is probably not going to be smiling or quietly reiterating what has already been said. Now he looks sterner, may raise his voice, and is likely to give some warnings such as "If you don't take care of this immediately, there will be consequences." This was the tone of many Old Testament prophecies, and rightly so. The people had been warned many times.

When delivering a prophetic word, those giving it generally have no idea whether this is the first or the fiftieth time the Lord has attempted to get through with His message. They must use the tone He desires and be careful not to come down too hard if they are not supposed to. God wants His purposes to be accomplished, and no one does a service when they pound somebody who does not deserve it. As a pastor, I (Joe) used to say, "Sheep can be sheared often, but they can only be skinned once." The biblical prophets provided correction, but they simultaneously told people what they could do to change. A prophetic message which is scathing and lacking in any hope or call to repentance and reconciliation is probably not indicative of God's heart.

The church still has a need for prophetic voices who will build it up, calling out holiness, encouraging what is right, and correcting as needed. They must "speak the truth in love" (Eph. 4:15) and care enough to confront. This is entirely different from those who are personally critical and irascible. No one with an attitude that is not grieving over sin or with a character not deeply loving should function in this capacity.

Shaping God's Preferred Future
Prophetic leaders are visionaries. After the Church is pure and ready to be used by God, He reveals His plans for the future. Prophecy shapes our thinking so we are enabled to imagine the future God wants for us. Walter Bruggeman, in his book The Prophetic Imagination, said, "The prophet does not ask if the vision can be implemented, for questions of implementation are of no consequence until the vision can be imagined. The imagination must come before the implementation. Our culture is competent to implement almost anything and to imagine almost nothing."⁴⁸

The prophetic keeps us hopeful and energized as the Lord proposes alternative futures.

God helps us visualize His preferred future. The prophetic is designed to keep us hopeful and energized as the Lord proposes alternative futures to what we humanly see. Jesus gave us the gift of prophetic ministry because the Church desperately needs God's shaping and direction. The Spirit affirms prophetically what we are sensing the Lord will do next. This provides security, internal preparation, and courage as we experience God's clear leadership.

An example of this was Agabus who is described in Acts

11:27-30 to be among several prophets from Jerusalem who came to Antioch where Paul was ministering. Agabus carried out his prophetic two-fold core task to hear from God and then communicate the message. Through the Holy Spirit, he predicted that "a severe famine would spread over the entire Roman world" (v. 28), and this did indeed occur during the reign of Emperor Claudius.

After hearing this prophetic word of a coming famine, the Antioch Christians gathered money to send to the believers in Judea, with this offering being delivered by Barnabas and Paul. The gift was appropriate since in the Roman Empire there was usually food available during a famine but at exceedingly high prices. With the help of this generosity, the Judean believers would still be able to purchase food. The prophetic ministry of Agabus was taken seriously and acted upon, with encouraging results. This time the Gentiles were blessing the Jews, a sure sign of on-going unity and mutual respect.

Agabus is also mentioned in Acts 21:10-12 when he came from Judea and met Paul while the apostle was on his way to Jerusalem. The prophet took Paul's belt and tied up his own hands and feet with it, declaring, "The Holy Spirit says, 'In this way the Jewish leaders in Jerusalem will bind the owner of this belt and will hand him over to the Gentiles'" (v.11).

When Paul's friends heard this, they tried to persuade Paul to avoid Jerusalem, but Paul did not listen to human advice. He knew personally he must go, and he responded by declaring he was ready not only to be bound but to die in that great walled city. Here again, the prophetic word was not in error; Paul was later bound and handed over to the Gentiles in Jerusalem. The prophecy didn't instruct him not to go—rather it seemed to be for the purpose of mentally preparing and fortifying Paul for what he already knew was coming.

Notice Agabus said exactly what God told him to say in both instances, no more and no less. He left it up to the hearers to make an appropriate response. A prophetic person should not add to or subtract from the word of the Lord but rather deliver just what God has given. Consider if Agabus had added his own words: "So you shouldn't go to Jerusalem, Paul." The Lord's plan could have been derailed, or it may have brought confusion to Paul. Instead, it generated resolution.

Paul was not surprised by this word Agabus gave him; however, when we ourselves are surprised by a word, the best thing to do is to set it aside for a time and wait. My wife, Renee, and I (Joe) have always said, "When in doubt, don't." A word may well come to pass, but time will tell. We should not do anything drastic. For example, we should not marry somebody based only on a prophetic word, nor should we move or change jobs if the Lord has not already been showing us about these potential changes. It is in the Antioch Church's favor that they collected the offering, even though the word was apparently a surprise. But in this case, they had nothing to lose—except they shared some funds which would bless the Judeans in any case. But God does not expect us to create havoc in our own personal lives or instruct others to do so if there is not an inner witness to a prophetic word.

How does the Church not lose ground, or better yet, how do we advance?

The guidance part of prophetic ministry also incorporates the church's relationship with society. The Spirit helps us interpret the times. We are presently in the midst of a highly fluctuating culture with huge historical shifts from modernism to postmodernism. How does the Church not lose ground, or better yet, how do we advance? If the Church chooses to answer this question merely through human reasoning, it will most assuredly fail in its paltry attempts. We don't have the intelligence to know exactly what is coming next, but God can reveal this to us prophetically.

We need individuals who will invest time in seeking God's plans. Amos 3:7 states, "Surely the Sovereign Lord does nothing without revealing his plan to his servants the prophets." Think about the implications of this. Whenever God does something, He shares it into the prophetic flow. Not utilizing the prophetic in the church severely limits our knowledge of God's intentions. A major path for discerning what He has in mind is cut off.

The Holy Spirit is our Revealer and Guide, using prophetic insight to clear the way, provide space for the new, prepare attitudes, and make everything ready. The Holy Spirit, through the prophetic voice, shapes His preferred future. God is completely aware of the future, and He wants to be the chief player. He calls the moves, instead of just reacting to the devil's scheming. If we are busy in our own smaller designs and not listening to Him, we will miss His greater picture. For these reasons, we need to include prophetic individuals at the planning table. Can you imagine how that would change today's church if regular pastoral staff meetings included humble, loyal, faithful, prayerfully apostolic and prophetic leaders as decisions are made?

As we enlarge our vision to God's larger Kingdom, we cannot remain content with things as they are. We are not satisfied keeping God's vision of tomorrow shrunken to the boundaries of the past or present. God wants us to do more than just get by. The prophetic functions to take us out of ourselves, into the future, giving us dreams and visions of how we can expand His Kingdom and make His name known. The prophetic has many methods and roles that will work together toward this end. The next step is to study some of these roles.

Chapter Six

God Uses Creative Prophetic Roles

*"I spoke to the prophets, gave them many visions
and told parables through them."*
Hosea 12:10

Prophetic ministry is both a normal and a wide-ranging function, and furthermore, it takes many forms. When we don't know what we are looking for, it's easy to miss where the prophetic is at work. To become more aware of what God is doing, the church must open its eyes to the many creative prophetic methods and roles that He uses to minister to us.

Those whom God taps out for prophetic work often receive their job description at the time of their calling. Sometimes several prophetic roles are combined. Although a huge variety of roles exist, we can only consider a few here. No two prophetic individuals will be the same, and the Lord will enable people differently according to the tasks He will assign to them.

The Communicator

One of the strongest prophetic roles is conveying a message through speech or in writing—the exact meaning of *nabi*, the most frequently used of the three Hebrew words for prophet. Those with prophetic voices are generally gifted communicators. They are interested in the meanings of words and are willing to do the work required to create a clear message. They take joy in selecting just the right term and are not careless about what they verbalize or write. The abilities to speak lucidly, think well, focus, compose, and carefully craft a flowing communication are invaluable assets to the Father when He anoints individuals prophetically. They may well have also developed good skills in persuasion, logical organization, and designing a memorable introduction and a moving conclusion. Individuals with good oratory know how to project their voice, enunciate clearly, and provide expression. They also model how to vary pace, use the right tone, and bring emphasis. Whether writing or speaking, they are particularly sensitive to their audience.

Just as God gives certain skillsets to those involved in apostolicity, evangelization, pastoring, or teaching, so the Lord usually blesses those working in the prophetic with highly honed communication skills in speaking, writing, or both. He often calls them to a secondary support role as a teacher and/or preacher. The prophetic is actually forthtelling, and this includes speaking forth, through a variety of means, what God chooses to share. Such individuals may be popular as conference speakers, and they may travel often since it is the Lord who places them where they may sow into the prophetic flow of ministry to the church.

Besides oral prophecy, writing is another means of working in the prophetic.

Besides oral prophecy, writing is another means of working in the prophetic. Books, for example, can fulfill a strong purpose. They can serve to move the church and individuals toward what the Lord desires. Sometimes one sentence, example, or chapter will redirect the way Spirit-led leaders focus their energy and ministries. Authors can be corrective, challenging readers in areas such as holiness, prayer, compassion, service, renewal of the spiritual disciplines, and loving God and others. They can stir up areas the Lord desires to re-emphasize or shore up matters that have been forgotten or are in disrepair in the church.

Many Christian authors report a sense of God-inspiration as they write. They are not likening their works to the Scriptures, naturally, but there is still a sense of the Lord providing depth and insight, revealing new principles the writer never saw before, or bringing to mind just the right word, phrase, or illustration. The Lord often shows them how to make an impact and bring a change or how to get across a challenging message. Prophetic leading and processes can be replete in certain books. We (Joe and Carolyn) could not have authored this book without the Lord's guidance, wisdom, and clear directive to write, and we believe the topics are on God's heart for the Church. He is wanting to ready believers—regardless of brand, label, denomination, or fellowship—for His second coming. He is desiring to pour out His Spirit in the end days: "Your sons and daughters will prophesy" (Joel 2:28).

Other writing besides books can also be prophetic. This can include blogs or articles in magazines and journals, or even something as simple as a note, letter, or e-mail. Having a word written out can be useful as the person has something to which they can refer back. Transcribing a spoken message to writing can be beneficial too. This way the word is accurate and does not rely on memory.

An excellent example of this happened at the beginning of the Argentine revival in the 1950s. An American missionary named R. Edward Miller locked himself away for day after day of prayer until he sensed a breakthrough in the Spirit. So many people got saved in the ensuing months, and a Bible school got started. Late one night a young student was in prayer in a nearby field, and the power of God came upon him. When he reentered through the school gates, his classmates awakened, sensing the fear of the Lord. They gathered together for prayer which lasted for over three months, often crying so hard as they interceded for Argentina and other countries that they stood in a pool of their own tears. The boy from the field that night started giving messages in tongues, and another young man received the interpretations, but he was frightened and ran out. Finally, they sat him down and transcribed them.

The messages and prophecies in this move of God included several words which seemed astounding. One was that Eva Peron (the popular wife of the president at the time) would pass away. She was young and it seemed improbable, so some outsiders made fun of this prophecy. Another word was that the largest soccer stadium in Argentina would be filled with people hearing God's word. This also appeared fanatical since at the time there were hardly enough believers in the country to fill a large stadium. Though many ridiculed the prophecies and there was a lag in time between these words and their fulfillment, all the prophecies that were written down (and are still available today) came to pass.

Even in the writing of this book, hand-written prophetic messages given to us years ago were found and re-read. Through the years of pastoral ministry, I (Joe) would from time to time receive well-meaning messages from congregants or even those I did not know. I would keep them to remember later what someone was speaking to me as God's plan for my life. Today, those words are now ringing true. How is it possible someone could write a message uniquely specific, or share something no one would expect, several years before it actually comes to pass? Spirit-led living, faith, and trust in God's holy Word leads one to recognize the Ephesians 4:11 gifts are not dead, but very much alive.

Good communication is a treasured value of moving in the prophetic.

Since good communication is a treasured value of moving in the prophetic, those called to this ministry should be particularly careful of their word choice and hone their skills in writing, composition, and orality. Although the spiritual gift of prophecy is often given at a spontaneous moment, much of the overall prophetic flow consists of individuals sensing God's message and the purpose He wants to accomplish and then pondering it over a period of time. The Spirit guides as they pray and consider the best way of communicating. As the author writes or the speaker composes the message, the Holy Spirit reveals new things, providing ideas for how to best go about opening people's hearts. Sometimes prophetic individuals test out the wording with a friend, assessing the impact and reactions so they can be ready to share the message as clearly and effectively as possible. While they talk it through, others make contributions and assist in the clarity. The Spirit uses our honed skills in many areas of ministry, and the prophetic is no exception.

One's choice of communication should be suitable and effective for the contextualized culture of those receiving the message. God spoke face to face with Adam and Eve (Genesis 3:8). The form of an angel was used when God dialogued with Abraham (Genesis 118:1-3). For Joseph, dreams and visions seemed most suitable to get his attention (Genesis 37:5). Moses was changed by the use of a media tool – the burning bush (Exodus 3:1-9). At Jesus' baptism, the Father God spoke with the sound of His voice and the appearance of a dove. For the Apostles, there were the tongues of fire (Acts 2:3-4).

Today, media tools such as television, internet, computers, and more can be the prophetic tools used for God's Word to permeate lives and families. Having served from the 2003 inception on the international Board of Directors for Unsion Television—an apostolic Hispanic initiative founded by missionaries Bill and Connie McDonald which offers a biblical world-view for news and content—I (Joe) have witnessed the thousands of people whose lives have been changed by God because of the prophetic witness offered through these media genres. Spirit-led sensitivity coupled with honed skills for clarity of God's message are keys for prophetic communication.

The Storyteller

One of the forms that prophecy often took with biblical prophets and still today is storytelling. In fact, between 50-65% of the Bible is narrative, and some say even higher. The fact that God so regularly spoke truth in narrative form is fortuitous since our present generation will tolerate this story form better than almost any other.

Storytelling doesn't point the finger. People relate to the character or plot and then realize the story is about them. Not as direct and "in your face" as some other forms of communication, storytelling hooks us with the account and then faces us with the truth. A story allows people to discover for themselves, so it manages to convey lessons and bring correction without sounding preachy.

Think about how Nathan the prophet used story to confront David about His sin (2 Samuel 12). He told a story of a rich man who had many sheep, and a poor man who had one little lamb that he had raised and loved. When the rich man had a visitor, instead of taking one of his own sheep or cattle to feed his guest, he instead took the poor man's only lamb and prepared it.

It was a carefully designed story, and David was engrossed by it. We are told David's anger burned against the rich man, and he said the rich man should die. Then Nathan is straightforward. "You are the man!" Story engages our emotions and our thinking. It effectually brought David to repentance and reestablished his relationship with the Lord.

Jesus Himself told countless parables. He pulled spiritual

truths from everyday life. Not only did these stories make his teaching remarkable, they also connected in a deeply profound way. Think about the parable of the Prodigal Son (Luke 15:11-31). Jesus could have taught, "God loves you so much that He will welcome you back no matter how sinfully you have lived. I will make this all possible by dying for you." Instead of such a direct prophecy, however, Jesus told the story of a boy who disowned his family, squandered his inheritance, came home to plea for mercy, but was surprisingly welcomed with open arms by his father who had watched daily for his return. Which is more powerful?

A story is something people remember better than the points of a topical sermon. It continues to work long after it has been told. We think about a story, apply it better to our own lives, and it continues to speak to us. Consider all that has been mined from the story of the Prodigal Son—how multi-faceted and rich it is.

Yes, crafting good stories and parables can be a prophetic work that changes us, corrects, or tells us what is to come. Consider the prophetic implications of Christ's parable of the fig trees right in the middle of his Olivet prophecy in Luke 32 or the parable of the great banquet (Luke 14:16-23). Look at the parable of the bridesmaids who went to sleep just before the bridegroom came (Matt. 25:1-13). Half of them had not come with enough oil and so missed getting into the wedding feast. What a sobering prophetic word this is. Jesus' stories have been told over and over again throughout the centuries, and we are still learning from them. Storytelling is a significant option for prophetic work.

The Dramatist

The Lord very often gave directions for dramatic and symbolic action to the biblical prophets for the purpose of emphasizing a prophecy and making it clearer. A dramatic production seeks to involve the audience, and the participants start questioning the actions, postures, and expressions of the characters, thus moving into deeper understanding. Prophetic drama made a difficult message or judgment more striking and easier to grasp. In the process, the prophet embodied the word from the Lord. They were used to bring the people back to a divine focus by their very actions.

So many examples exist of God giving the prophets instructions for dramatic acts which they were to perform as a vehicle for

His message. One example, of course, is Hosea whose relationship with his prostitute wife, Gomer, is a symbol of God's relationship with Israel. Though Gomer and Israel were unfaithful, God would take them back. The book of Hosea makes a dramatic call of repentance to Israel. This dramatization undoubtedly cost Hosea deeply.

> *Multiple scriptural accounts show the prophets getting instructions for dramatic acts.*

Jeremiah was directed to put on a yoke (Jer. 27). Since the prophecies he had delivered did not persuade the people to submit to the Lord, they would now be taken over by King Nebuchadnezzar, signified by the yoke. The word from the Lord was therefore to yield tamely to avoid the destruction of their country. Of course, Israel did serve Babylon for nearly fifty years, but Jeremiah wrote down all the disasters that would then happen to Babylon. He sent Seraiah to read the scroll to the Babylonians, tie a stone on it, and throw it into the Euphrates River, thereby indicating that Babylon would rise no more (Jer. 51). These are graphic demonstrations designed by God to accompany His words.

Ezekiel was yet another prophet used in prophetic dramatization. God, the director of the drama, gave these instructions in Ezekiel 12:1-3a:

> Then the word of the Lord came to me saying, "Son of man, you live in the midst of the rebellious house, who have eyes to see but do not see, ears to hear but do not hear; for they are a rebellious house. Therefore, son of man, prepare for yourself baggage for exile and go into exile by day in their sight; even go into exile from your place to another place in their sight..."

We see here that God uses prophetic drama because people don't see or hear well, thereby missing what God has been trying to communicate. When Ezekiel carried out the dramatization, they were all astir, asking him what his actions meant. Can't you hear them? "Hey, Zeke, what do you think you're doing? Why all that baggage? Going on a trip, are you? Where?" Notice after Ezekiel completed the assigned drama, he then received words from God that shared clearly what He meant. Now the Lord had the peoples' attention. He then gave Ezekiel yet another drama: eating his bread and drinking with trembling, quivering, and anxiety (v. 17-20).

Prophetic dramatization also occurs in Jeremiah 13 when the

prophet is told to buy a new waistband, then go to the Euphrates (a long journey some weeks away) to bury it. Sometime later, God sent him back to get it, now a ruined cloth. Next the word of the Lord came to Jeremiah personally that the belt represented the ruined pride of Judah and Jerusalem. We have no reason to believe Jeremiah ever shared this particular experience with anybody. In this case the prophetic dramatization about the belt seems to be geared to the very heart of the prophet himself: "Then the word of the Lord came to me...." (Jer. 13:8).

A symbolic act accompanied prophetic explanation in other scriptures, such as 1 Kings 11:29 when Ahijah the prophet met Jeroboam and tore his new cloak into twelve pieces, giving Jeroboam ten. We can also look at Isaiah who would probably be arrested today for the prophetic action that accompanied a prophecy in Isaiah 20. Read it for yourself along with Ezekiel 4 where the prophet dramatized a siege of Jerusalem along with the dire straits the people would have to endure.

With the considerable usage of dramatic action God ordered to accompany prophecy, those working in the prophetic now should seek to be open to directives from the Lord regarding similar demonstrations today. Contemporary culture is open to drama and such God-directed expressions may well be ways the Lord would like to get people's attention and speak to them. Most surely this is not to be a dramatic undertaking that comes from a person's own imaginations, any more than a spoken word. It has to be a mandate from the Lord, otherwise it is worthless, false, and maybe even crazy. Rather, we must listen to God's precise directions and follow those carefully.

The Seer

Recall that most of the Hebrew words for prophet were often translated as "seer." It indicated a person who saw what God wanted to communicate. One of the words, Chozeh, was derived from the same Hebrew root from which we get our word for vision, meaning that the prophet received the message through a divinely initiated vision. In Numbers 12:6 God said, "When there is a prophet among you, I, the Lord, reveal myself to them in visions, I speak to them in dreams."

A seer had such an important role that people came to them for advice and direction. Seers still exist today, though often they are not recognized, sought out, or heeded. A person called by God for this ministry often receives wisdom and guidance in the form of a visualization. Many of the Old Testament prophets introduced their writing by using words associated with seeing because the visions were a fundamental part of their message. For example, the Book of Isaiah opens with this: "The vision concerning Judah and Jerusalem that Isaiah son of Amos saw during the reigns of Uzziah, Jotham, Ahaz and Hezekiah, kings of Judah." He was basically referring to his whole book right from the start as a vision containing the things he had seen. Likewise, Ezekiel's opening line declares, "As I was among the exiles by the Chebar canal, the heavens were opened, and I saw visions of God" (Ezek. 1:1). Here he uses the plural word "visions," making sure we know this was a normal part of his life. We often talk about "hearing from God," but with the seers and prophets it was also very much about vision.

> *So often in Scripture the prophets received a strong visual element in their communications from God.*

So often in Scripture the prophets received a strong visual element in their communications from God. The Lord asked prophets what they saw, interacting with them regarding the vision and its meaning (See Jer. 1:11-12 and Amos 8:1-2). God required the prophet to reflect upon the meaning of the images and to discern God's message and purpose. This must have been quite challenging when the visions were difficult to interpret such as John's Revelation, or when Zechariah saw a giant book soaring through the air (Zech. 5:1-2) and Ezekiel saw a strange collection of half-animal and half-human figures (Ez. 1:4-14). Other prophets received a vision of God Himself, enthroned in His glory and accompanied with surreal images and various symbols.

The prophets were accustomed to receiving visions, dreams, and visuals. These will be discussed more in the "How" chapter that follows. First, however, we need to realize the normality of these prophetic processes. Habakkuk 2:1 provides an example: "I will stand at my watch and station myself on the ramparts; I will look to see what he will say to me, and what answer I am to give to this complaint." Note Habakkuk talked about "looking to see" or "watching to see" what God will say. Obviously, God's message can be discerned visually, and if we want the prophetic to flow, we should be open to seeing as well as hearing.

Even Jesus talked about seeing. In John 5:19 Jesus said, "Very truly I tell you, the Son can do nothing by himself; he can do only what he sees his Father doing, because whatever the Father does the Son also does." The Father didn't just tell His Son what to do nor did He only speak to Jesus about what He was doing. Rather He showed it to Jesus and then the Son followed suit. They were truly one, and Jesus both heard and saw. Obviously, if we want to be like Jesus, we should be open to sharpened spiritual vision!

The seeing role ought to be something we are willing to grow and flow in.

As we spend time with the Lord, He shows us broader perspectives of what is happening in His Kingdom. Our sight is enhanced and sharpened. The seeing role ought to be something we are willing to grow and flow in. Sometimes it is challenging to understand what is being shown to us. Still, it is not always ours to decipher but to specifically deliver as God directs.

An example of "seeing" still makes me smile. At the Christian university where I served as a Vice President, I (Carolyn) had a group of students who came weekly to my office for prayer and intercession. One of the young men I remember was a great guy, wholly committed to the Lord and very sensitive in the Spirit. Actually, he was a converted warlock; but oh, how he now loved Jesus! He had become an amazing prayer warrior. One day as we ended our prayer time and the students were trailing out, I felt nudged by the Lord to call him back and found coming out of my mouth, "Hey, Bob (name changed), why aren't you dating?" This was unusual for me since I was not really a matchmaker.

He chuckled, "Oh, no! God has already been speaking to me about this, but I don't think any girl would be interested in me."

"Oh, come on, you are depriving some nice gal from having a wonderful companion!" I said. "You need to pray about this."

That Friday night was our monthly All-night Prayer Meeting, and he sat down beside me and asked for prayer about the situation.

As I was doing that, I had a vision. I saw him walking in a field on a beautiful autumn day. He strolled into a grove of golden leaved trees with their bows spreading over a clearing and the sun sparkling through. On the ground was a log with little white periwinkles around it.

I have to admit to being puzzled. What did that vision have to do with his dating life? I hesitated, wondering if I should even disclose it. But I had learned long ago that it was not mine to figure out, but my job was to be obedient and share.

So, I said, "I just had a picture come to me. If this means nothing to you, please disregard it and think maybe it was the pizza I ate for dinner." We both laughed. Then I told him the vision, and he started to cry. He said, "This place exists just as you described it." (I was happy for that!) "It is on our family farm, and it is my favorite place in all the world. I feel safe there, and I think God wants me to know that I will feel this way when I start dating." Ahhh! I could never have helped him with this myself! God did it in such a beautiful way, and I was so happy I had taken the risk to share the vision, even though I didn't understand it and felt awkward. When we work in the prophetic, we need to be willing to look like fools and to step out in sheer faith. We aren't required to have everything defined and revealed ahead of time. By the way, he asked a girl out the next week, and they got married soon thereafter.

The Administrator and Shifter

Another role for the prophet is often as an administrator who helps lead an organization and bring about change. An example of a prophet in this capacity is Isaiah. He served four kings of Judah (Isa. 1:1). What are the odds so many different leaders would allow the same person to be their scribe? I doubt it could happen today. In his role, Isaiah was at the table, privy to the big issues. He had influence, serving at the very heart of the decision-making process of the kingdom. Each king wanted him to remain in his position, probably because Isaiah was a prophet, sensitive to God's leading and providing crucial insight and direction. His prophetic understanding allowed him to offer input that guided the kingdom.

One of Isaiah's greatest contributions was that he could see the big picture as few others did. He gave more Messianic prophecies than any other prophet, and he was constantly concerned about the breadth of God's Kingdom. When individuals have both administrative and prophetic giftings, their inclusion at the leadership table of churches, as well as district or national offices, is invaluable.

Another value of prophetic administrative gifting includes leading out and advocating for change.

Another value of prophetic administrative gifting includes leading out and advocating for change. Various prophetic core traits lead to this, for example, the desire to see people be transformed and fulfill God's best for their lives. Also, sensing what God wants to do in the future is a natural frontrunner for planning and preparation activities. Many prophetic individuals speak out about getting things ready or changing the systems, structure, and programming so they are more conducive to God's future work.

Along with this goes the God-given prophetic ability to shift things. Various times when I (Carolyn) preach, I feel a certain church is not heading in exactly the right direction for what God intends. This may regard an outdated emphasis, an imbalance, or a neglect of something important. Perhaps what they are doing is not at all wrong morally but rather just not the best path for what God ultimately wants to accomplish. Sometimes as I preach such a message, I feel in the Spirit the shifting of gears—like a big machine is grinding its mechanisms and moving differently. I can even feel the release of tension when people accept the change the Lord is proposing. I believe what I have described is part of the prophetic gifting from God through which His power can flow to accomplish a change.

It is as if the prophetic individual puts a hand on something, figuratively speaking, and God gives it a quarter turn, sending it off in a new direction. The release is tangible. I have very often had pastors come to me after I preach and say things like, "I have been preaching about this topic for weeks. I never told you. How did you even know? But today for the first time, something released in the Spirit. This was exactly what we needed."

Likewise, very often through the years the Lord has given me (Joe) direct words of wisdom, change, purpose, the need for repentance and renewal, or new direction for individuals in a private consult. I can feel the Spirit altering their course of actions and transferring His directives to their hearts and minds, as they yield and allow God to transform their circumstances. For some it was to write a book, for others to enter the ministry, and for many to leave their worldly ways and accept Christ as their personal Savior—as was the case just this past week at a funeral I preached, when I asked an adult grandson if he was ready to leave his former ways and accept new life in Christ. He said, "yes," and I had a local pastor with me lead the young father in prayer as he accepted Christ at his grandfather's funeral. It is amazing to see God direct the prophetic gifts to bring about change. God wants to bring many shifts in churches and individual situations as the prophetic is released.

This shifting is part of the unique ministry of the prophetic.

Prophetically, it is impossible to take the credit for these things. God leads in the sermon or teaching, lends His transformational words and power to the situation, and He Himself makes the shift in the spiritual realm. His spoken words bring things into being. This shifting is part of the unique ministry of a prophetic individual, and this is why we need the five-fold ministry working together. No particular one of the five-fold gifts is designed to go it alone. Each role has important and specialized work it has been anointed to accomplish.

One aspect of flowing in transformational work is that, whenever possible, God likes to give the word in a positive format. Prophetic people model and explain what the final outcome will look like. Listen carefully to a seasoned prophetic minister because they may not be railing against something but rather drawing people to its opposite. The Lord generally starts with the positive and tries to bring about change kindly. Then if the person or church does not listen, the message will become more definitive and correctional.

The Old Testament prophets clearly had a large tool box as they worked in the prophetic. They would not take out a hammer and squash someone if tweezers would do. An example of this is when Nathan "shifted" David to repent of his sin and come back into relationship with God. Instead of scolding and hammering away at David about his sins, Nathan simply tells a story and says, "You are that man." Even after David's great sins (both adultery and murder), David still had a soft heart. The tweezers were sufficient. There were hard consequences yet to endure, but the repentance and transformation came quite quickly.

Jesus spoke gently to the Samaritan woman at the well, and she and the whole town shifted (John 4:4-26). On the other hand, He strongly rebuked the Pharisees: "You whitewashed tombs!" (Matt. 23:27-28), and still they refused to change. Shifts come only as we carefully listen to whatever process God chooses. When done His way, He will bring about the changes that are necessary. The prophetic is often used to cut the path, bring forgiveness and healing, pave the way, and initiate God's plan. Prophetic individuals simply need to be very cognizant of the many tools in their toolbox and select just the right one for each occasion.

Chapter Seven

Prophetic Worship and Poetic Communication

*"I wish that all the Lord's people were prophets
and that the Lord would put his Spirit on them!"*
Numbers 11:29

Two areas of prophetic release deserve their own concentrated study: 1) prophecy in worship and 2) poetic communication, closely aligned to songwriting, speaking, and writing. Both of these are integral to the prophetic flow and serve as effective vehicles for God to speak to us.

This chapter includes discussion of a few simple poetic elements used in scriptural prophecy, like comparison. God used these so often, in fact, that we dare not leave out these important methods. First, however, focus is on the fact that poetic prophecy was often sung.

Prophetic Songs in Scripture

Much of the Old Testament's poetry could be sung. Some think of poetry as being complex and veiled, thus making it almost too obscure to decipher. However, poetry can be simple with memorable rhyme, and when set to music, it becomes even more powerful. This is true of the poetry found in hymns and various spiritual songs.

We can often recall lyrics to a tune we haven't heard for years. In fact, music tends not to erase in our minds though we lose other capacities. People with advanced dementia, for example, can often croon all the words of a song, even if they can barely speak. When prophecy is set to music, we remember it better, and it has a greater impact upon us. We know this was utilized by the Old Testament prophets because of what Samuel prophesied to Saul after anointing him as King:

> "After that you will go to Gibeah of God, where there is a Philistine outpost. As you approach the town, you will meet a procession of prophets coming down from the high place with lyres, timbrels, pipes and harps being played before them, and they will be prophesying. The Spirit of the Lord will come powerfully upon you, and you will prophesy with them; and you will be changed into a different person. Once these signs are fulfilled, do whatever your hand finds to do, for God is with you" (1 Samuel 10:5-7).

Samuel said that in the midst of the prophetic song, God's Spirit would come mightily upon Saul, and this experience was to be so powerful, it would change him into a different person. What an effect of prophetic music!

Saul's experience with prophetic song would change him into a different person.

The Psalms were the hymnbook of the Old Testament Jews. They were poetic, and one could put a metronome to them and recite them in time. With this backdrop, it is notable that the Psalms are a major depository of Messianic prophecy concerning the First and Second Coming of Jesus. Sixteen of the Psalms are distinctly Messianic, and all but three of these are quoted in the New Testament, pointing to fulfillment of the prophecies being in Jesus.

Other prophetic Old Testament songs exist such as the song of Moses in Exodus 15:1-19, sung after the Lord delivered the Israelites at the Red Sea. Here Moses moves into the prophetic as he tells how there will later be victory as they come into the Promised Land. In the next two verses Miriam is named as a prophetess, and taking up a timbrel, she sings in worship and dances with all the women.

Deuteronomy 31:19-22 has instructions from the Lord to Moses, telling him to write down a song and teach it to the Israelites. The song was to provide prophetic information about the future (see Deut. 32 for the song itself):

> "Now write down this song and teach it to the Israelites and have

them sing it, so that it may be a witness for me against them. When I have brought them into the land flowing with milk and honey, the land I promised on oath to their ancestors, and when they eat their fill and thrive, they will turn to other gods and worship them, rejecting me and breaking my covenant. And when many disasters and calamities come on them, this song will testify against them, because it will not be forgotten by their descendants. I know what they are disposed to do, even before I bring them into the land I promised them on oath." So Moses wrote down this song that day and taught it to the Israelites.

Still other prophetic songs exist in Scripture such as the Song of the Vineyard (Isa. 5:1-7), a Song of Praise which Isaiah prophesied would be sung in Judah (Isa. 26), the Joy of the Redeemed Song (Isa. 35), and the Song of the Suffering Savior (Isa. 52:1-12). Likewise, other prophets used songs, including Jeremiah, Hezekiah, and Ezekiel. We are also encouraged in the New Testament to sing (Eph. 5:18-19).

The Joy of Prophetic Worship

Prophecy and music were coupled so frequently in Scripture, it becomes apparent that this poetic and musical vehicle for prophecy is being quite underused today. Has the contemporary church become too professionalized and scripted to allow God to move prophetically in song during our services? We must not let this happen!

Those who are songwriting and leading worship should be aware of the potential impact of their poetic message. Through testimony, Charles Wesley impacted millions over the last few centuries with his poetic metaphors detailing candidly the work of the Holy Spirit in his life. His hymn "And Can It Be That I Should Gain" has an example of his memorable imagery:

> Long my imprisoned spirit lay
> Fast bound in sin and nature's night;
> Thine eye diffused a quickening ray,
> I woke, the dungeon flamed with light;
> My chains fell off, my heart was free,
> I rose, went forth, and followed Thee.[49]

Likewise, as worship leaders bring people into God's presence, the Lord can use them to sing or speak a prophetic word. I (Joe) served as a minister of music for a number of years. Often, I would stand at the pulpit as a song's last chorus closed, sensitive to

God's direction and voice, sometimes in what some might consider deafening silence, but when, in reality, God was so apt to speak. Other times, encouraging musicians and congregants alike to linger in God's presence, we would sing "a new song" before the Lord and intently focus on genuine worship. When the prophetic pastor leader gives time to wait upon the Lord, God is welcomed, and His presence inhabits the praises of His people. Numerous times during these special moments, I witnessed altars become filled with hungering saints, praying for family members, repenting of personal sin, and being renewed and dedicated to the things of God.

Additionally, a spiritual gift of prophecy or tongues and interpretation often comes from the congregation during genuine worship. Some have mused this is a learned habit. Why does it so often seem to come during this particular time? It appears more likely, however, that meaningful worship puts us all in a better place to hear from God. He speaks to us as we are praising Him, and music has always been a means God uses to move us and change us. Why wouldn't He use the moments while we are focusing on Him to speak to us and through us? Of course, this is not the only occasion God moves prophetically, but it can certainly be a viable prime time.

As we (Joe and Carolyn) have each experienced the exuberant praise and worship of other cultures (many from the Argentine church or the African church, etc.), we readily recognize the shallow nature in much of the worship offered from the West. Sorrowfully, the delight and vigor of amazing grace is lost when it is no longer amazing. Though one cannot judge the individual worship styles of others, as some are very quiet or internalized in their personal expressions, many in our western culture sing and worship as if it is an adopted hour in our week, rather than a remarkable encounter with the living God.

A "new song" is an intimate message that ushers in God's presence.

In deep worship, God often gives both the message and the music in a song that is new to everyone, even the musicians. This is spontaneous as inspired by the Holy Spirit. A new song ushers in God's presence, since it is an intimate message and process akin to receiving a personal, hand-written note with just the right words at exactly the correct moment. This cannot be pre-planned.

Such ministry from the Lord can be very powerful. Often people are strongly convicted, healed, and delivered during prophetic songs.

Five of the Psalms command us to sing a new song to the Lord, as does Isaiah. When we give ourselves to a prophetic flow, new songs are more apt to occur. "Christ in you" sings to and through us. This interaction is shown in Zephaniah 3:14-17 where Israel is told to sing and shout, but God Himself will also be rejoicing with singing. What a beautiful picture of what happens in prophetic worship. We sing; God sings:

> Sing, Daughter Zion; shout aloud, Israel!
> Be glad and rejoice with all your heart, Daughter Jerusalem!
> The Lord has taken away your punishment, He has turned back your enemy.
> The Lord, the King of Israel, is with you; never again will you fear any harm.
> On that day they will say to Jerusalem,
> "Do not fear, Zion; do not let your hands hang limp.
> The Lord your God is with you, the Mighty Warrior who saves.
> He will take great delight in you; in His love He will no longer rebuke you,
> but will rejoice over you with singing."

It takes faith to allow God's songs to become our songs. Worship leaders must be willing to step out and release new songs, forgetting their pride and the uncertainty of where the unknown song will go. As they forge ahead with fresh words and melody from the Lord, God will work powerfully and touch lives.

This also happens as we sing in the Spirit (1 Cor. 14:15) where God gives a tune to the accompaniment of tongues. It can occur individually or in a group, with the group generally harmonizing in parts—the Lord giving different lines to different people. It is most beautiful. As we lay aside our self-consciousness and allow the Lord to sing through us all, God moves in a precious way. The best place to start is in private worship, which then encourages a person to move in the freedom of the Spirit during corporate worship as directed by the Lord.

As 1 Corinthians 14:15 indicates, we should sing both with our spirit and with our understanding. Sometimes the Lord will give a prophetic word and provide the melody ahead of time rather than moving spontaneously during worship itself. The songwriter may feel led to craft a tune to fit the words, thus pre-composing a prophetic song to teach others later. This method is also viable, and the Holy Spirit can work greatly in this matter as He guides the songwriter in advance. All of this is good.

Musical Instruments and Artistic Expression: Awakening Our Spirit

Musical instruments can also play a role in the prophetic work. Various instruments can be so attuned to the Spirit that they usher in the presence of God in a powerful way, awakening the individual spirit. I (Carolyn) have heard drum beats in Argentina that resonated so deeply in my spirit that they changed and strengthened me, opening my ears to God's voice. The beat was like hearing the very heartbeat of God.

The beats seem to melt away sin and strongholds, heal emotions, and empower for action.

Such a sound can contain so much life-giving grace that it leads worshipers into the very presence of the Lord and transforms them. The beats seem to melt away sin and strongholds, heal emotions, and empower for action. This is not a learned drumming method but rather a God-given work of the Spirit. I have talked with others who have had the same experience with drums and other instruments in various parts of the world.

We already mentioned the instruments used by the prophets who met Saul (1 Sam. 10:5). Another example is 1 Chronicles 25:1-8 that indicates not only voice but other musical instruments may be used in prophetic song: "David, together with the commanders of the army, set apart some of the sons of Asaph, Heman and Jeduthun for the ministry of prophesying, accompanied by harps, lyres and cymbals." The passage goes on to provide specific names of the musicians and explains that the sons of Asaph were "under the supervision of Asaph, who prophesied under the king's supervision" and the sons of Jeduthun were "under the supervision of their father Jeduthun, who prophesied, using the harp in thanking and praising the Lord." Then, in verses 6-8, it mentions the sons of "Heman the king's seer" and states:

> All these men were under the supervision of their fathers for the music of the temple of the Lord, with cymbals, lyres and harps, for the ministry at the house of the Lord. Asaph, Jeduthun and Heman were under the supervision of the king. Along with their relatives—all of them trained and skilled in music for the Lord—they numbered 288. Young and old alike, teacher as well as student, cast lots for their duties.

The musical instruments were obviously an integral part of the prophetic message. All musicians should be ready to accompany prophecy, including a new song. In Argentina during the revival, I (Carolyn) heard distinct instruments besides the drums which God used to complement certain prophecies. The music emphasized the words. Once I was quietly delivering a prophetic word to an individual, and the person leading with his synthesizer half the room away started a prophetic song which contained the exact same words that were coming out of my mouth.

Notice in the scriptural example above, the large number (288!) of those who were trained and skilled to use instruments and prophesy musically—so many, in fact, that they drew lots for God to select those He wanted. Age did not matter since young and old alike were chosen, the teacher along with the students. I would love to see this method used today. What am amazing worship team!

Observe too that the sons were under the supervision of their prophetic fathers. This oversight provided proper guidance and assurance that prophecies were given accurately. The prophetic fathers were supervised by King David himself, the master musician and prophet. This nugget speaks of a teachable spirit, submission, obedience, and accountability on all levels. How beautiful this is.

I (Joe) was in college when I encountered a radical experience with the Holy Spirit and a newfound relationship with Christ. Prior to my accepting a call to ministry, while attending the university on a partial music scholarship for trumpet, I focused my attention on the musical genre of instrumental jazz. During those early years of growing in the things of God, usually twice per week in good weather months, a young keyboardist and I would find ourselves in the university's "free speech" area playing music for the thousands of passersby: a selection of contemporary Christian arrangements ascribed with our own improvisational accompaniments. There were times no one would stop to listen. Other times a handful would linger. And, there were the occasional moments when a decent crowd would assemble on nearby lawns or lean against concrete pillars, as if a prophetic expression were billowing in the wind, calling them to hear the voice of God.

Worship extends to many parts of a service. It can also incorporate other artistic forms such as poetry reading (which can be prophetic), drama or dance, or painting and other art media. These all hold the possibility of being a prophetic vehicle. I (Carolyn) have seen artists painting during a service who definitely were using visualization/seer traits and methods for prophetic purposes. My wife and I (Joe) have hanging in our home a beautiful portrayal of Christ painted by a parishioner during one song of a worship service. The artist painted it upside down, then turned it over at the closing chorus of the song. It was a powerful point to that moment of worship. No one could tell what he had been painting until he turned it right side up. So it is with God's work—His masterpiece of our lives—as we are so often unable to recognize that He is at work at all, while we are enduring the challenges of life's journey. But then He turns it "right side up," and everything suddenly makes sense. The whole painting and lesson were His prophetic imagery at work.

So many artistic individuals inhabit our pews, but unless they are involved in music, they often are under-utilized in their expressive gifts. We are narrowing down the prophetic pathways if we do not allow their God-directed creativity to emerge. The Lord ordered that numerous craftsmen and artists be utilized in the building of the temple. He enjoys many forms of beauty and art.

We need to be open to the gifts of sanctified imagination and artistic skill that God wants to use under the guidance of His Holy Spirit. They must be under His rule, however, and their purpose must be to bring glory to Him. When individuals—sometimes on purpose and sometimes inadvertently—draw attention to themselves in any artistic ministry, the genuine prophetic work and heart of worship are squelched as eyes are taken off God and transferred to the artists or their art form. This is of the flesh and not able to be sanctified as holy unto the Lord. Church leaders who are Spirit-inclined will discern this and not let such people lead the congregation in worship activities.

May the Lord help us be more concerned with a prophetic flow of worship than with entertainment.

Since music is an artistic path we regularly utilize, may the Lord help us be more concerned with a prophetic flow of worship than with entertainment. If everything becomes too professionalized, music can be set so tightly that God cannot minister through the prophetic whenever He chooses. As we allow the

Lord to lead real heart worship (not just sing a few songs without thinking), the atmosphere can shift and the way is prepared for the prophetic to be released, both during musical worship and afterwards in the preaching of the Word.

Often, while I (Carolyn) am in worship before I preach, the Lord shows me things prophetically and reveals new aspects He wants me to share with the congregation. I have often had music teams, whom I have never talked with before the service, play songs which completely match my message. Their prophetic music literally ushers in the prophetic word. This is encouraging to all as we see God is speaking to us communally. May we let the prophetic ministry flow throughout our services as God leads.

God the Wordsmith

God crafts His words in songs, poetry, teaching, and writing. Jesus Himself was called the Word: "In the beginning was the Word, and the Word was with God, and the Word was God" (John 1:1 NIV). The Trinity loves to design good communication.

Poetry comprises one-third of the Bible and the majority of the Old Testament.

God's skill shines throughout the Bible. The language used by the prophets is, on the whole, best described as poetic. Poetry comprises almost one-third of the Bible[50] and the majority of the Old Testament, some saying as much as 75%.[51] Most of this does not readily leap out to us as poetry because of translation issues where much of the rhyming, beat, and other poetic aspects are necessarily lost. Even when poetic methods come through the translation, we do not always recognize them as such. We cannot all become poet laureates, but our awareness of some of these simple techniques is useful—both to properly interpret biblical prophecy and to welcome the Holy Spirit's incorporation into prophetic ministry today.

Why would God choose to utilize poetic methods to speak to us? Poetry is packed full of imagery which forms mental pictures, leads to deeper understanding, and stirs the emotions. Our godly imaginations are moved by these sensory images which awaken not only our intellects but also our hearts. Poetry is an integral part of songwriting and thereby makes its way into music and worship, all of which combines to move us deeply.

Poetic "figures of speech" abound in prophetic proclamations in Scripture and also today if we know what we are listening for. Some people don't "get poetry," but let's check out a small handful of poetic devices used in prophecy.

Simile is when two things are compared using the word "like" or "as." These are all through Scripture, but the prophet's beautiful verse in Isaiah 1:18 (NASB) is a great example:

"Come now, and let us reason together,"
Says the Lord,
"Though your sins are as scarlet,
They will be as white as snow;
Though they are red like crimson,
They will be like wool."

See how these similes provide us with an amazing promise and prophetic word regarding the experience of salvation. They fill out the meaning.

Metaphor also compares two things but does not use "like" or "as." The comparison shows unusual relationships which provide insight into what God is saying. When prophet John the Baptist calls the people "an evil and adulterous generation" (Matt. 12:39; 16:4), he is readily understood since so many Old Testament prophets used this comparison of adultery (the book of Hosea, Ezekiel 16:38, Jeremiah 3:20 to name only a few). John paints the metaphor of Jesus as the bridegroom (John 3:29), and Paul says the Church is the bride, communicating a great deal through this metaphor which threads throughout Scripture. The seriousness of our union with Christ and prophetic warnings against committing adultery all take on extended depth with such a powerful comparison. Metaphor is one poetic form that rings with our present generation because it is indirect and makes us think.

Symbols are material objects used to illustrate spiritual truth such as the mercy seat, candlesticks, oil, the brazen serpent, the altar, yokes, manna, the ark, and so on. Even animals are used as symbols such as Jesus' donkey, a lion, wolves, the dove, sheep, the ox, and dogs. There are so many symbols in the Bible that we could barely remove them without leaving huge, gaping holes.

Both **parable** and **allegory** are extended metaphors or

similes. Prophets, including Jesus Himself, often utilized both. God directed the prophet Ezekiel how to give a prophecy: "Son of man, set forth an allegory and tell it to the Israelites as a parable" (Ez. 17:2). Ezekiel was then told to prophecy using metaphors for kingdoms of that time—eagles (Assyrian supreme god), breaking off the top of the tall cedars (king of Jerusalem), and being carried away to the land of merchants (Babylon). These meanings were clear, given the symbols of the times. We too can communicate prophecy through such poetic wordsmithing, as we are guided by the Spirit.

The sounds of the selected words themselves are also utilized throughout Scripture to heighten meaning. **Alliteration** is the recurrence of similar sounds in successive words, such as in Isaiah 1:18-20 where recurring "k" sounds in the original Hebrew wake up the listener to the message of salvation. **Assonance** is recurring sounds in accented vowels like in Isaiah 53:4-7 where the "u" sound occurs fifteen times, heightening the grief. **Onomatopoeia** uses word sounds to point to the realities of what they describe as in Isaiah 42:14 where guttural sounds and usage of the letter "p" remind us of a woman in labor.[52] Review the listed scriptures and ponder the power of God's careful word selections.

One last poetic device to explore is the use of **hyperbole**. This is an exaggeration used for emphasis as in Jer. 9:1: "Oh, that my head were a spring of water and my eyes a fountain of tears!" The word "hyperbole" comes from a Greek word meaning "to deliberately throw outside or inside a marked line for effect." The hyperbole is not to be taken literally since it is designed to exaggerate or diminish outside of fact. It is not a lie because the hearer or reader is supposed to understand that it is meant to be a hyperbole if they have any sense of the poetic at all. The exaggeration is useful to shock people out of their lethargy. Certainly, we are not to make up something for the pure joy of shocking others; that is ridiculous. But hyperbole can do a good job of waking people up when it is clearly led by the Holy Spirit.

Jesus used hyperbole quite often. One example is John 6:30-59 where Jesus stated that He Himself was the bread of life. The people started grumbling about this, and He told them to stop it. He then went farther yet, stating that those who have eternal life will eat His flesh and drink His blood. Of course, people were shocked. They took Him literally, thinking He must mean actual cannibalism, and they started to argue "sharply" (v. 52). Even His own disciples said this is a "hard teaching" (v. 60), and many of them turned back and stopped following Him (v.66).

Prophetic understanding can be challenging to discover, but God wants us to think about His words.

Why would Jesus do this? Prophetic understanding can sometimes be challenging to discover, but God wants us to think about His words, not immediately take offense at them. Jesus was teaching a deep truth here, foretelling the possibilities of eternal life for those who believe and foreshadowing our understanding of the Last Supper. This is profound and needs to be peeled back by layers to find the truth. Hopefully no one will write off the truth that God speaks to us merely because we do not understand it right away. We need to ponder and discern, being careful that we do not behave like those poor disciples who chose to walk away from the Messiah Himself.

One final example to throw in regarding Jesus' use of hyperbole is Matthew 5:29-30. Jesus said if our right eye causes us to stumble, we should pluck it out, or if our right hand causes us to stumble, we should cut it off and throw it away. Another shocking comment! Obviously, He doesn't mean this literally or all Christians would be blind amputees, but He is urgently earnest about the fact that we have to go to almost any lengths to remove sin in our lives and come to salvation. The hyperbole awakens us and leads us to think about the seriousness of sin.

As we combine known techniques of rhythm and rhyme, of beats and figures of speech, we end up with meaningful songs and messages that "stick" and make people think. God desires these results for the prophetic. His words are important and should not be glossed over or listened to half-heartedly.

Purposes of the Poetic in Prophecy

One of the commentaries says, "All of these techniques, which are of course nearly impossible to reproduce in English translation, invigorate the linguistic medium, excite the imagination, and thereby increase the impact of the prophetic message."[53]

This is so accurate! In order for people to pay attention and get the full effect of what God is saying, a variety of communication devices needs to be utilized. When we speak a prophetic word, we are careful to speak loudly enough for the intended group to hear, perhaps turning toward them, standing up, moving to an aisle, getting to a microphone, or otherwise thinking through how we are delivering a message. We speak clearly, provide emphasis and cadence, and watch our pacing. In the same way when we write down a prophecy or speak it, we should be aware of what kind of communication techniques God may want to use to make the message memorable and distinctive.

Besides helping prophecy be unforgettable, poetic techniques have a wide variety of other purposes including emphasizing the message, condensing it, empowering it; they can even hide a message so the answer has to be discovered.[54] A metaphor, for example, may actually make a message somewhat obscure, but Jesus consciously did this quite often. He was apt to answer questions with parables and similes rather than giving direct answers. Why did He do this? Well, it makes people think and ponder the message later. They are inclined to "mine" it, so to speak, to mull it over, since it has layers of understanding which can be discovered. A good metaphor or symbol holds hidden truths and is rich in continued teaching.

The many poetic aspects of language are used throughout Scripture and evidence God's great care in utilizing words carefully to communicate to His people. God leads us to use careful word crafting in preaching, writing in all genres, drama, songwriting, and other vehicles for prophetic ministry. We just need to be more open to the import of words and let the Spirit guide us.

Chapter Eight

The 5 W's and H

> *"I keep six honest serving-men*
> *(They taught me all I knew);*
> *Their names are What and Why and When*
> *And How and Where and Who."*[55]
> Rudyard Kipling

Delivering a prophetic word takes a truckload of discernment. So many considerations demand attention. Sometimes well-meaning people hear a word from the Lord but are then inclined to blurt it out immediately right where they are. Instead, the work has only begun. We must discover the Lord's choice of timing, delivery, purpose, place, and methods. For this, we can take some lessons from the field of journalism.

Every reporter knows that the lead for their news stories must include the five W's and H: Who, What, When, Why, Where, and How. These questions are the key ones to ask in order to uncover the complete story, and this is also the case for anyone working in the prophetic. After receiving a word from the Lord, we have to stop and think. What should we now do with this word? To whom should it be given? What exactly is to be said? When and where should it be released? Why is the Lord wanting this word to be given; what are the purposes and results He wishes to accomplish? Finally, how is it to be delivered?

Often known as the 5W1H, these questions are even part of research, rhetoric, and police investigations. People have asked them since classical antiquity because these queries help gather data and observations, problem solve, and draw correct conclusions. In the case of prophecy, we must gather important information to discover what the Lord wants us to do with the word He gave us to share.

When?

A little proverb helps us understand the importance of "when": "Like apples of gold in settings of silver [i]s a word spoken in right circumstances" (Prov. 25:11 NASB). A huge mistake for budding prophetic types is to assume that when they receive something from the Lord, it should be released immediately, belted out loudly and formally. Many alternatives present themselves.

Perhaps the word should not be shared at all. The message may be only for the person who received it. If the word is resonating deeply and personally and the receiver is attached to it, this may well be the case. The best approach then is to wait and sort this out before conveying it to anyone else.

Since a primary task of the prophetic person is prayer and intercession, it's quite possible that the word is meant to be prayed over. With one of the main goals of the prophetic being to come alongside the purposes of God, the effects of prayer can be most efficacious in bringing about what God desires. As a person intercedes, God is at work, altering situations and drawing people to Himself. If the situation shifts through prayer, then the word may never have to be shared at all.

At times an urgency from the Spirit nudges to share the word then and there. In this case, various nuances of timing still come into play. We are instructed in 1 Corinthians 14:40 to do things decently and in order: "But everything should be done in a fitting and orderly way."

A church which is open to the work of the Spirit will allow appropriate places for the use of the lingual gifts of the Spirit. God actually owns the space in a service, and it is not ours to commandeer. He has priorities and plans. If there is no space left for Him to enter in, this defeats our desire of honoring the presence and activity of the Lord in our midst. When song follows closely upon song, choruses are repeated five or six times, and then the offering and sermon, the service can be so tightly compacted that the Spirit cannot breathe. Add to this that many churches still offer a reading of the bulletin or personalized announcements, taking even further time from the worship service. And oh, how we need the wind of the Spirit!

There were times as I (Joe) pastored, when I would step to the platform and do nothing but wait. Most often the tangible presence of God would manifest and settle among us. When you've witnessed it, you'll never forget it and always desire it again. These are moments when various gifts of the Spirit, including prophecy, are vital and rich.

Though God may choose to speak in these consecrated spaces, it is perfectly acceptable to be still in His presence, and just know He is there. A quiet spot does not necessarily mean it is time for a lingual gift. Parishioners must realize that not every space is meant for a word of prophecy; the Spirit is not filler. If that begins to occur, the Spirit-sensitive pastor will need to recognize quickly the realities of guiding and teaching those within a church open to the gifts.

Instructions for the use of the prophetic in a church service are provided in 1 Corinthians 14: 29-33:

> Two or three prophets should speak, and the others should weigh carefully what is said. And if a revelation comes to someone who is sitting down, the first speaker should stop. For you can all prophesy in turn so that everyone may be instructed and encouraged. The spirits of prophets are subject to the control of prophets. For God is not a God of disorder but of peace—as in all the congregations of the Lord's people.

Those who are leading services or groups or even committees should have sensitivity to the Holy Spirit in perceiving when a word might be forthcoming from someone else. As the prior verse clearly states, they should stop. Many do this so well, even allowing for that time of silence as the people rest in the presence of the Lord. The "first speaker" (which may include singing) should not feel they must hold the floor but should sense what the Spirit wants to do in using others. If the Spirit is not given privilege to interrupt or speak, then people may not "be instructed and encouraged" (v. 31). This would be desolate, not to allow God to do His work.

Prophetic individuals should be patient, however, if a pause does not occur right when they think they have received a word.

They are to be serene and wait. The Spirit will not forget what He desires to do and say. One receiving a word from the Lord should not interrupt another person who is speaking already since this would be jarring and disorderly. Even if a prophetic word is ideally supposed to occur but those in charge do not pause, the Lord will provide another way, another time. The ones with the prophetic word must not get angry because someone else seemed to lack sensitivity. In actuality, perhaps that leader was more astute to the Lord's timing than they are and the word is meant for later or for someone else. Even if not, God is able to get His word across so no one should ever become riled or haughty as if they are more spiritually astute than someone else. The Lord will be at work. "Make every effort to keep the unity of the Spirit through the bond of peace" (Eph. 4:3).

The Spirit will not forget what He desires to do and say.

Discovering the right time to release a word can be challenging at times. Once while traveling I (Carolyn) visited a church in Alabama I had never previously attended. The Lord gave me a word during the worship time, but there was no place to deliver it during the rest of the service. I didn't get upset, but instead I held the word quietly in my heart. An altar time followed the service, and I felt I was supposed to just sit still and pray. After the altar time came to a close, I sensed I should go up, introduce myself to the pastor, and tell him I felt I had received a word from the Lord. He called all the other staff pastors and deacons over and asked me to share it. The timing was perfect. The pastor told me afterwards that I was the third stranger in a single week who had come to them with the exact same word. The Lord was definitely speaking and confirming His direction!

Confirmation is a timely gift of the prophetic. It is a powerful work of God in the lives of those desiring to flow in His perfect will. Renee and I (Joe) had resigned our first ministry assignment after only one year because of a strong inclination from the Lord that He was about to open a new door which would impact our lives and others for years to come. We had no idea what that door would be and in a full act of faith resigned our present position without yet knowing where we would be going. I don't propose most to do that, but in this case, we had a clear sense it was God's will to simply trust Him.

Within three weeks of our resignation, there were three confirmations given to me by individuals not connected to one another that we were to inquire about full-time ministry in a certain direction. The confirmations proved true and were timely. That specific direction ended up being the church we served as youth pastors, worship pastor, associate pastor, and ultimately lead pastor until the time of our transition to the office of state denominational superintendent. Prophetic confirmation encourages the person receiving it as well as the one releasing it, since the prophetic individual also realizes he/she has heard from the Lord and that the Spirit is guiding both the giver and the receiver at the same time.

The Lord will orchestrate the perfect moment for the prophetic word to be released.

When exactly should we release a word we have received from the Lord? The delivery of a word may be immediately, but it may also be further on in the service, later in the day, in the subsequent week or month or year, even. The Lord will orchestrate the perfect moment, when the person or group is most receptive to the word and prone to take the action He desires.

Why would the Lord give a word before He wants it delivered? Often it provides for a period of preparing the hearts and spirits of everyone to receive what God wants to say. His plans are always perfect, and He makes a path so the words can be issued in the "fullness of time" (Gal. 4:4). As we peacefully wait on the Lord for the correct discharge time, we learn to trust, rest, not speak prematurely or rush things too quickly. He will open the door and make the path smooth.

God tells Habakkuk, "For still the vision awaits its appointed time; it hastens to the end—it will not lie. If it seems slow, wait for it; it will surely come; it will not delay" (Hab. 2:3 NAS). The word is released in God's timing, and it comes to pass in His chosen moment. The person used in the prophetic is not responsible to force a way to give a word nor to fulfill it. Quite the contrary; God's got this.

Who?

Before a prophetic word is released, another question must be answered. To whom should this word be delivered? In the example mentioned in the last section about the church I (Carolyn) visited, my lingering for the perfect time also allowed for the leaders to hear that particular word. Learning more about the situation later, I don't believe it was meant for the entire congregation, even though the Lord gave it to me earlier in the service. The Spirit's guidance for "when" also allowed for His plan to unfold regarding "who" should hear this specific guidance and affirmation of direction.

Sometimes a person inexperienced in the prophetic feels emotion in the moment, but emotional sensation should not be confused with a move of the Spirit. We need to use our minds as well as our emotions and to consider who should hear this and under what circumstances.

Emotional sensation should not be confused with a move of the Spirit.

Some words are meant to be conveyed to just one person instead of an entire group. If a word is personal or corrective for an individual, then this is almost certainly the case. I (Carolyn) remember once when I was again traveling and attended a church I had never visited before. As I sat in the service, I felt like the Lord gave me a word of knowledge that the pastor was seriously considering resigning but that God was about to turn things around at the church. I sensed I had a prophetic word for the pastor and probably his wife, but it was not anyone else's business right then. How was that supposed to happen?

To make the matter more difficult, the bulletin announced that the pastor and his wife were leaving for a two-week vacation right after the service. I would be gone from this area in just several days. What was I to do? The chance of having time with the pastor after the service was practically nil. I prayed.

When it was over, I stayed in the pew for a while. The pastor came up, and having discovered who I was, he asked if I would have lunch with him and his wife. I told him I would really like to, but wasn't he starting his vacation right away? He assured me they had time for lunch. In the restaurant, at a quiet table we were given, I had the chance to deliver the word. It was in normal conversation, but they knew it was from God. They wept and said they were indeed planning on finalizing their decision while they were away, but now they could enjoy their vacation because the Lord had just showed them what to do.

The prophetic word should be delivered carefully. Even who can overhear should be noted when doing altar or other types of ministry. Recently, while I (Carolyn) was worshipping in church, the Spirit gave me a prophetic word for a young man sitting nearby. It had to do with his call into the ministry, so I went up to him after the service. He was visiting my home church, so I told him who I was so he would not wonder about the person delivering the message. I addressed him, but his grandmother was next to him and she was a committed member of our church, so I felt it was all right for her to overhear. His mother came over and heard the last part and after I started down the aisle, she ran to me with tears and told me what I had shared was something the Lord had already revealed to her. She provided other personal circumstances, and I was able to minister to her as well. I wouldn't have let an unrelated crowd hear this word, but these were people who loved the boy, could debrief with him regarding it, and could assist in his next steps, so God gave release for them to participate.

Once in a while the Lord asks a prophetic individual to give a word to someone in authority over them. Though this can be frightening for a variety of reasons, they still have to obey the Lord. Their leaders also need to hear God's direction, encouragement, affirmation, and even correction at times.

Prophetic workers should never deliver a prophecy to a person they don't care for. This is also the case for someone with whom they are angry. Under such circumstances there is too much temptation to add their own feelings, both in tone and words. Those functioning in the prophetic never should let their own emotions get mixed up in a pure word from the Lord. If there is such a danger, let someone else give that word. This is important whenever there are strong feelings of any kind involved, whatever they may be. This includes jealousy, early feelings of love, contempt, prejudice, haughtiness, desire to impress, anxiety, frustration, and so forth.

Sensitivity regarding the person or group who receives a prophetic word is something to cultivate. Obtaining the guidance of the Spirit on these choices is critical.

Where?

Some people think the main, and perhaps even the only, place to deliver a prophetic word is in a church service. The places where God wants to work, however, are limitless. A word from the Lord can be delivered during a service in the sanctuary or afterwards at an altar time. But it can also be delivered in other places in the church such as a youth group, in a Sunday school class or other teaching time, in a committee meeting or Board room, or even in the church kitchen or parking lot.

In fact, prophetic words can be given outside the church building in a restaurant, in a home Bible study group, with your children in their room, at work, on the sidewalk in your neighborhood, with a stranger in a store aisle, in the hospital, in the nursing home, at a soccer game, or anywhere.

If we shut up the prophetic inside the church, then we limit God's work.

Just like the other currents of the church (pastoring, evangelization, teaching and discipleship, and the apostolic) can happen anywhere, so can the prophetic. We are to care for others, be ready to share the good news, and be prepared to answer questions and help people to grow. Likewise, words from the Lord should flow in normal conversation to encourage, confirm, and edify.

Thinking in this way broadens the options of where someone can hear a prophetic word. People are everywhere, so many in pain and wishing for direction, healing, and help. Isaiah 55:10-11 (NASB) says this:

> For as the rain and the snow come down from heaven, and do not return there without watering the earth and making it bear and sprout, and furnishing seed to the sower and bread to the eater; so will My word be which goes forth from My mouth; it will not return to Me empty, without accomplishing what I desire, and without succeeding in the matter for which I sent it.

When the prophetic word flows, God undertakes to accomplish what He yearns to do in people's lives. If we shut up the prophetic inside the church, then we limit God's work. Once I (Carolyn) was driving home and noticed a man walking along the street in Minneapolis. I felt I should stop because the Lord had a word for him. I had to turn my car around, but I obeyed the quickening of the Spirit.

I approached the man and told him I felt God wanted to share a message with him. I looked down and noticed he was carrying something which looked like a Bible. He acknowledged it was and that he was heading down the street to the church for an evening Bible study. I told him what I sensed the Lord wanted to say to him: That God was pleased with him for how much he was sharing his faith at work. That the Lord saw not many appeared to listen and he was getting frustrated by this and thinking of giving up the attempts. But the Spirit told him people were being affected more than he knew and that he should continue to share the good news because it would make a difference in these people's lives, and he would see much fruit.

He shook his head and said he could hardly believe it because this was exactly how he was feeling, and he had been praying about what he should do. He said how encouraged he was that the Lord would speak to him like this, and he would continue for sure. We both rejoiced. God's word did not return to Him empty but accomplished what pleased Him (see Isaiah 55:11).

God had His word delivered on a city sidewalk, and there are many such stories. The Lord is all around us, and the prophetic can flow in multiple scenarios. We need to have our ears open to listen for when God might be speaking to us in all sorts of situations. Life is exciting; God is at work at all times and in all places!

What?

Another consideration relates to "what" God desires to say. This is an important area. No one should add one's own interpretation or ideas to what God wants to impart. If we are about to deliver a prophetic word, but we personally have strong opinions about it, there is a danger that we will get our own ideas entangled with it. We already talked about emotional strings, but our rational thinking can get intertwined also.

Does it matter if this happens? Yes, indeed it does. Jeremiah 23: 16-18 refers to false prophets who speak on their own. Prophetic individuals should never share their own ideas as if they were from the Lord. They must not give a message that will please people if the Lord wants to say something different. Likewise, they should not be hard when the Lord wants to be gentle. Christians should never let their own thoughts or experiences affect their delivery of a word.

It is important to stay neutral and let God speak exactly what He wishes.

If those giving forth a prophecy are familiar with the one to whom they are prophesying, then they should be careful not to mix in what they think they already know about that person. It is important to stay neutral and let God speak exactly what He wishes. They are also not meant to interpret what the Lord has said and add that to the Lord's words.

At times, if God reveals a word ahead of time, prophetic workers have the opportunity to think too much about it and comingle their own ideas. They must be careful about this, tearing down vain imaginings and pretensions.

Those familiar with prophetic release realize that there are many valid ways God provides them with His message. Sometimes He gives it all at once and sometimes only a little at a time. When the Lord reveals a great deal of the content of the prophecy ahead of time, they start to speak as the Spirit releases it. At other times they do not know what the word will be. Maybe they only get a phrase or a sentence that keeps going over in their minds. God nudges them to move ahead and speak in faith. In some ways this is unnerving, for they do not know if much will come out at all. However, those called to the prophetic must never add their own thoughts to fill in. If the message is short, even just a phrase, let that be it. He asks us to deliver that which is authentic, not elaborate. If more comes, then share it.

What about how the person accepts the content of the prophecy? So often it is a confirmation of what the Lord is already speaking to that individual. This makes the delivery easy because there is ready acceptance and understanding. But what happens when the person is puzzled by the word? This does not necessarily mean the word was incorrect. Time will tell. The receiver should weigh the word and if it is not particularly understandable, then they should be advised to "set it on a shelf" and wait and see.

One time I (Carolyn) was back in Argentina, walking on a shopping street with a friend. A young man who worked in a store ran out onto the street as he recognized us. He said to me, "When you gave me a word about five years ago, I thought, 'That just isn't going to come to pass! It is too far out there.' But," he continued, "it has all happened exactly as it was prophesied. I just wanted to let you know how accurate the message was, even though I didn't believe it at the time."

Some words which are given can take a few months, or years, or even a lifetime to come to pass. What has been said can ultimately be accurate. In preparing the writing of this book, I (Joe) reviewed a number of prophetic words given me in the 1990's and early 2000's. As I recognized the truth today in my life of words given to me decades ago, I again stood in awe of a God who so cares about His children that He speaks at times knowing we do not understand, yet leading us to trust the beauty of His omniscience.

Many prophecies have conditional "if" clauses attached to them. If the hearer does this, then God will act in a certain way. Some prophecies do not come to pass because the person does not do their part. They may rebel against the Lord and go their own way. The prophecy would have come to pass if the person had been obedient, but when he or she is not, then the word of the Lord is aborted and the promise is lost.

Some years ago, willing to step out in faith, I (Joe) went to a younger associate pastor—upon the resignation of the lead pastor of his church—and shared with him and his wife in a perfectly natural conversation that I strongly sensed he was to be the next pastor of the church. He opted not to pursue that route and the church soon thereafter elected another pastor from out-of-state. The elected pastor ultimately found challenges, conflict, and a near church split before finally resigning and leaving the pastorate open once again. The associate pastor was then elected lead pastor. Timing and personal choices (the "if" clauses) relegate the outcome of words of this nature.

An example of this is 2 Chronicles 7:14: "If my people, who are called by my name, will humble themselves and pray and seek My face and turn from their wicked way, then will I hear from heaven, and I will forgive their sins and heal their land." Notice that God makes a promise of what He will do in the future, but the promise hinges upon whether or not we do our part.

Why?

What are the purposes and intentions the Lord has in delivering His prophetic word? Why is He wanting to speak to us? We cannot always answer this question, but many times we perceive what He hopes to accomplish.

Often God is excited to share the future with us, to bless us with hope and faith, or to prepare us for what is coming. His purpose may be to strengthen and encourage us. Sometimes He wishes to affirm what He has already been speaking to our hearts, making sure we know that we have heard accurately. This can provide us with assurance and courage.

> *When people are not open, it feels like running into a cold, hard wall.*

At other times God wants to correct us as His children. Those delivering prophecy can often sense the openness of those they are addressing. Some, on the other hand, may be cold and hard, being unwilling to hear what the Lord wants to say. When this happens, giving the message feels like running head on into a hard wall! Even if it is a word of correction or pointing out sin, the Lord's purpose is to bring healing and restoration. God hopes for repentance, cleansing, and renewal of the relationship between Himself and the individual. He wants people to turn their hearts toward Him as Ninevah did when Jonah confronted them or like David did when Nathan told his prophetic story.

It must not have been easy for Nathan to confront his king with such an accusation of sin. Many called to work in the prophetic are willing to share if the prophecy is one of ease and compliments. However, it is more difficult if God's purpose is to bring repentance and change. If prophetic individuals want to be popular, they may be tempted never to give a corrective word or do it "lightly" with a smile.

This is akin, however to knowing a friend has cancer—even being capable of performing the surgery to remove the tumor—but then refusing to do so. Indeed, sin is like a cancer that will spread if it is left unattended. (See Leviticus chapters 13 and 14.) Yes, it may take a knife to cut out the tumor and that hurts, but if this isn't done, the sin will spread and death will result. Prophetic individuals dare not skip this highly important work. Who wants a cancerous church?

In order to come to grips with actually delivering a message of correction, the prophets of old found themselves weeping, being emotionally gripped by the need to share a hard word. They were pained to give the message, but they knew they must do so no matter the consequences.

Today the bearers of prophecy sometimes find themselves beaten up by persons receiving God's message and perhaps by someone in authority who is not discerning what the Spirit wants to say. May God provide discernment to church leaders so they will recognize genuine prophecies, even if corrective.

I (Carolyn) have sometimes been called upon by the Lord to deliver what I would consider a painful word. Once I had to warn someone that if they (I do not want to indicate a "he" or a "she") did not take care of a particular situation (the word was specific but I will not explain here), then they would lose their ministry for the rest of their lives. I was heartbroken before the Lord for this individual. I did not want to share this word. I had no actual proof of what I was sensing and that made it all the more terrifying. But I burned with this message for several months and interceded.

Finally, the Lord gave me a time and an opening. I was faithful to the message, but the person did not repent. They were very angry, and I paid quite a price for my obedience to God. A number of months later the situation came into the light. They lost their ministry and never got it back to this day. I know for a fact that they cannot say before God that He did not warn them or try to help them in their temptation.

When God's desired outcome of a prophetic word does not come to fruition, it is a sincerely tragic thing in God's eyes. He wants to help us, and He will do anything to take care of the cancer spread. It is up to us to soften our hearts, not to take lightly or make fun of a sincere prophetic word, and to let the Lord accomplish all He desires... everything... every little piece.

A similar pain occurs when sin is not at issue, but people resist simple change or God's directions. They are comfortable where they are at and do not want to move out of it. I (Carolyn) have had times when I preach or give a prophetic word, and I sense a strong wall. The people do not want to hear or to take it in and learn from it.

I sense God at times with a battering ram... and His message gives a push on the door... and then another one... and another one. There is a rush at it... all in the Spirit, but the person or the church refuses to budge. They don't want to hear. They won't listen. The purposes God has for the word are not accepted. This is a grievous feeling: knowing that God is contending but man is holding out against it. Oh, that we will open up the door to real prophetic work in our midst and let God in!

Chapter Nine

The H: How

"In the beginning was the Word, and the Word was with God, and the Word was God."
John 1:1

*"Come, Holy Ghost, for, moved by thee,
thy prophets wrote and spoke:
unlock the truth, thyself the key,
unseal the sacred book."*[56]
Charles Wesley

How to deliver the word that the Spirit gives is another challenge for the prophetic voice. As we have seen, prophecy may utilize such vehicles as speaking and writing, the seeing function of the seers, administration, and worship. These all have implications for exactly how to deliver a message from the Lord.

An individual called to move in the prophetic does not have to get up tight or sound officious in delivering the message. After all, other gifts of the Spirit are not pre-announced in a formal way. A person simply offers a prayer for healing or shares a word of knowledge, speaks wisdom, and works in other areas such as administration and hospitality for the benefit of others, and the Spirit flows and moves into the middle of it all. The gifts of the Spirit are "supernaturally natural" and so is the working of the prophetic within the Church and outside of it. Let's explore more key details about how this can work.

Interaction in the Meeting Room

One way the prophetic can be delivered in an unpretentious manner is during meetings. A great many prophetic leaders have a place at the table. They are administrative or invited into leadership, and God opens the doors for them to have influence. A great example is the prophet Isaiah.

We have probably all been in a meeting where everyone is talking and generating ideas, but nothing seems to be quite the right answer. At the ideal moment, someone speaks up and shares something so insightful and perfect that everybody knows immediately it is the correct decision. Others wonder, "Why didn't I think of that?" But those who are sensitive realize God's wisdom and leading. This is really the natural working of God through the prophetic; He correctly guides us into the future and provides security and a sense of peace and agreement.

One who delivers prophecy has the responsibility to pray and hear from God about the direction of an organization or church, a program, or mission. A mature person will pray before and during a meeting, staying connected to the Spirit and holding until it's the correct time to say something.

> *The mouths of prophetic servants need to be under the care and control of the Spirit.*

If individuals often used in the prophetic tend to chatter away with their own opinions and ideas, then when they have something to share from God, His words will not be so easily distinguished. They must learn to rope in their own thoughts and concentrate on what God wants to speak into a situation. The mouths of prophetic servants need to be under the care and control of the Spirit. They should keep their communication restrained until God wants them to open their mouths, learning to listen a lot both to others and to God. Out of the depth of this unseen core of being, God is able to rise up and make Himself known when and as He chooses.

Just as cautious speaking is important in good prophetic communication, so is careful listening. Those in a meeting likewise need to pay attention to what God wants to say so they can recognize His direction when it is stated. Many times, we can be so attached to our own opinions that we miss hearing the leading of the Lord.

Receiving God's prophetic guidance means that everyone must be sensitive to the Spirit. It helps if the group prays for a while ahead of the meeting. This attunes everybody to God's voice, setting the stage for His intervention as people open up to the revealing of His plan and take the focus off their own agendas.

The release of the prophetic flow should be desired in board meetings, in committees, in planning and business meetings, and in department discussions and staff meetings. People tend not to be as sensitive to the prophetic flow in these settings as they might be in a church service. However, the decision-making and strategizing points desperately require prophetic input from the Lord, and God very much wishes to provide that.

Although Christians may pray about a meeting and its outcome, they often neglect sensitivity to the Spirit in the meeting itself. I have heard people grieve if they could not or did not deliver a prophetic word in a church service for any number of reasons, but we ought to be just as grieved at the lack of the prophetic in our church meetings.

If we all fanned our desires for this, then I believe we would see it happen more regularly and freely. We would also experience fewer decision errors which result in wasted money and ineffective efforts. When we choose methods not in God's plans, people expend a great deal of energy and receive little fruit in return.

Release in Preaching and Teaching

Both preaching and teaching are also potential vehicles for the prophetic to flow. Prophecy involves forth telling or proclaiming as well as foretelling. Isaiah said, "The Sovereign Lord has given me an instructed tongue, to know the word that sustains the weary" (Isa. 50:4). What a fantastic picture for godly verbal communication! When preaching, teaching, or speaking in any context, prophetic workers should exhibit an instructed tongue. The result will be a special word providing stamina and sustenance to the weary, along with direction, motivation, and encouragement. Teaching and preaching can change people's lives.

Of course, all sermons and teaching are not entirely prophetic. Nonetheless, the pastor and teacher should be aware of the opportunity to sow words directly from God's heart. While they are speaking, the Spirit often says something they had not prearranged or intended. God takes over the message, and words come forth like they do in a prophecy. Often there is the sense that this is for somebody in particular, and after the message, a person will come up and say those words were directed at their exact situation.

The pastor/teacher should be alert to opportunities for sowing words directly from God's heart.

Likewise, the same sense of Spirit directive can be aimed at a whole church body, where God speaks forth what the church needs to hear. This happened in the book of Revelation when John was prophesying to the church at Ephesus. Specific congratulations were shared, but then there was a necessary and serious correction (Rev. 2:1b-7a).

Good preaching and teaching speak truth—both positive and/or remedial—as the Spirit leads. Once I (Carolyn) was in another state speaking, ending up some state-wide services with preaching Sunday morning and evening in two different churches. As I prepared, I knew what God wanted to say to those two churches was very different.

I sensed clearly that the morning church was at a crossroads, getting ready to elect a new pastor. No person had even told me this about the pastor leaving, but the Spirit prepared me. If the search committee made a selection only by the resumés they received and went with human logic for selection, they could well miss the person whom the Spirit had chosen. Those results, I perceived, could be disastrous for what God intended for that place. The word delivered was one of seriousness and forewarning. God led me to preach Scripture which applied generally to the church, and then I felt directed to write a more specific word of prophecy to the search committee for private delivery. The pastor had indeed just resigned, but God knew all along what was happening and guided the message along prophetic paths.

The evening service was entirely different. I felt the Lord wanted to compliment them for many things, and He gave me specific verses which would allow His commendations to come forth. Here again, when I arrived, I witnessed with my own eyes that which the Lord had revealed to me through my message preparation.

Those who preach and teach need to be particularly sensitive to what God wants to say in specific situations. These are opportunities for the Lord to speak to individuals, a group, or the whole church. We dare not pull out just any old sermon; we need to do the work of hearing from God for a fresh word and be open for His prophetic direction.

Visions and Seeing

Another "how" for the delivery of a prophetic message is through the sharing of visions or pictures. One of my (Carolyn's) doctoral students, Joshua Scroggins, said in his book *Awakening the Christian Imagination*: "When God wanted to capture the hearts of the prophets, He first went for their imaginations. He spoke to them in visions, symbols, and dreams. The prophets then went after the imaginations of the people. The prophetic imagination distinguishes the prophet from other people."[57]

Scroggins then quotes Abraham Heschel, one of the leading Jewish theologians of the 20th century, who wrote, "Like a poet, he [the prophet] is endowed with sensibility, enthusiasm, and tenderness, and above all, with a way of thinking imaginatively. Prophecy is the product of poetic imagination."[58]

In order to develop the prophetic in our lives, we must let God awaken our pure imaginative thinking. We should be open to seeing and hearing metaphor, parables, stories, and symbolic acts. I (Carolyn) once stood on the isle of Patmos in the cave where John received his vision recorded in Revelation, and I wondered. What must it have really been like to see all that, to sort through those many symbols? What an experience! How did Isaiah feel during His visions of what would happen to Judah and Jerusalem or when he saw the Lord?

Often today God gives pictures or visions for people to share for prophetic purposes. Most of these are not at the magnitude of John's experience or Isaiah's, but they can guide others nonetheless. They can be a simple picture that explains something or gives instructions. An example is Ananias receiving a vision to go to Straight St. in Damascus and respond to a picture God had already given to Saul (Paul) in which Ananias came and laid hands on him, restoring his sight (Acts 9:10-19). Visions can have import.

A spiritual picture can provide healing, hope, and faith for what God intends to do.

As I (Carolyn) pray at the altars for people, I sometimes receive a picture that so clearly describes what is happening with a person or what is about to happen. Such a picture, when conveyed, helps the individual to see confusing circumstances more clearly. It summarizes and condenses the issues which may seem overwhelmingly complicated to the individual. The picture may also provide healing, hope, and faith for what God intends to do. Visions can speak to people in very personal ways, often sharing what only God and the individual know.

I have, for example, seen a broken and wounded heart which God was stitching together with pretty ribbon, tying a bow, and providing lace, flowers, and other decoration. It was stunningly beautiful! The meaning is readily obvious because we can understand the symbols.

Another time I saw a person walking along in the mud on one side of a dark and barren building with weeds and thistles along the way. Their head hung low, they walked slowly like the burdens of the world were on their back, and they could barely keep going. Then they came to a corner, turned it, and found a lovely meandering path with beautiful flowers and sunlight. God led me to prophesy that they were right at the corner, about to make the turn, and it was happening right then and there, at that very moment. Tomorrow would be different.

God uses visuals to encourage people, give them optimism, and prophesy the future. I believe He would give more to us if we would allow our sanctified imaginations to receive them.

The Scripture is full of visual images, including ones from Jesus Himself. This encompasses examples like hiding your candlestick under a bushel basket (Matt. 5:15) or telling us we are the salt of the earth but if we lose our saltiness, we can't be made salty again and will be trampled underfoot by man (Matt. 5:13).

Jesus also speaks to Saul in Acts 26:14: "We all fell to the ground, and I heard a voice saying to me in Aramaic, 'Saul, Saul, why do you persecute me? It is hard for you to kick against the goads.'" This visual comes to my mind often when I am struggling against something which I know is within the will of God. The picture quickly speaks to my discontent and how I will continue to hurt myself if I keep kicking like an ox against those sharp goads, trying to get out of my yoke.

This, in fact, is one of the great things about a vision or visual. Like many other prophetic methods, it is vivid. Andy Stanley, in talking about church vision statements, said they needed to be kept simple so they were memorable, and things that are memorable are then portable.[59] We take them with us. They stick.

Dreams

An additional "how" for delivering prophecy is through dreams. A prophetic dream is when foresight or insight is gained through a supernatural night vision. In Scripture, people received prophetic dreams which they understood, but at other times prophets and others were needed to provide the interpretation. The godly prophets were then able to accomplish their task of foretelling as God revealed it to them, often resulting in great impact on whole kingdoms and cultures.

Many instances abound in Scripture where God gives prophetic dreams and interpretations.

Many instances abound in Scripture where God gives prophetic dreams to people including ungodly kings (Joseph's Pharaoh in Gen. 41 and Nebuchadnezzar in Dan. 2) or average men (like Laban in Gen. 31:24) or patriarchs like Jacob (Gen. 28:10-22) or prophets like Daniel (Dan. 7:1). In Pharaoh's case, Joseph's prophetic interpretation saved the kingdom. And then there was poor Daniel who was rather on the spot when King Nebuchadnezzar told all his wise men that they either came up with both his dream and the interpretation, or he was going to chop them all up into little pieces and demolish their houses (Dan. 2:5). God showed Daniel both the dream and the prophetic interpretation, allowing Daniel to give glory publicly to the one true God and draw the king's attention to God's great power and nature (Dan. 2:20-23).

At other times the dream was so clear that an interpretation was unnecessary as in Gen. 20:1-6 where Abimelech, the King of Gerar, is warned in a dream that Sarah is Abraham's wife, not his sister as Abraham had claimed. Or when Joseph was told in a dream to take Mary and Jesus to Egypt (Matt. 2:13) to escape Herod.

Prophetic dreams still occur. There are many reports in these times about Muslims who have dreams of Jesus, showing Him to be the Savior. Often in places where access to the gospel and the Word of God is limited, people will have dreams leading them to places where they can hear the truth.

If individuals feel like they have had a prophetic dream, they should always check it against the Scriptures. Once I (Carolyn) had the wife of a seminary student tell me that she was free to commit adultery because she had a dream that it was okay. I told her, of course, that this dream was assuredly not of the Lord, and she should stop in her tracks and go back to her husband.

If the dream does not contradict Scripture, we must still ponder it and submit it to the Lord. Sometimes people ask me to help interpret their dreams. I do like Daniel did with Nebuchadnezzar. I ask for time to pray and seek wisdom and understanding. If I do not receive insight from the Spirit, I am not going to say I know what it means just by using my own head. That can be a great failure for sure. Daniel told Nebuchadnezzar that God had shown him the interpretation: "No wise man, enchanter, magician or diviner can explain to the king the mystery he has asked about, but there is a God in heaven who reveals mysteries. He has shown King Nebuchadnezzar what will happen in days to come" (Dan, 2: 27-28). The Lord wants to be in charge of everything, both the dream and our understanding of it.

Prophetic Prayer

Prophetic prayer is another means by which prophecy can be delivered. The prophetic aspect is to pray in accordance with the understood revelation given by the Holy Spirit. This can occur in personal prayer, when praying for another person, or in corporate prayer.

In its simplest form, prophetic prayer is not just sharing what is on our mind, but rather is predicated upon learning what is on God's mind. When we pray prophetically, we lay down our own desires and burdens, depending on Him to tell us what is on His agenda. We align our prayers with the will of God. In any prophetic release, the first task is to see or hear from God before speaking the message He wants to share, and the same concept applies to prophetic prayer. Praying from a personal prayer list is a legitimate way to pray, but in prophetic prayer, we are seeking what is on God's heart and praying this forth.

In prophetic prayer, we are seeking what is on God's heart and praying this forth.

Recently, a friend told me (Carolyn) of an experience which perfectly demonstrates prophetic prayer in ministry. A man had come to her and stated that his daughter needed prayer. She did not know him or the daughter and he did not share any details, but my friend sensed some things in the Spirit and prayed for the girl accordingly. My friend later learned that the man was very encouraged because she had prayed in faith into the exact circumstances of what was going on, giving hope for the future. This is a great example of prophetic prayer coupled with a word of knowledge.

God's very words from Scripture can also be shared in prophetic prayer because then we are definitely praying according to His will. An example is Nehemiah who was grieved about the destruction of the walls and gates in Jerusalem. For days he sought God—mourning, fasting, and repenting. He quoted God's promise to Moses that He would return the exiles to their homeland if they shifted their hearts back to Him. Nehemiah prayed prophetically about the future of his people, and God opened the door for them to return (Neh.1).

Likewise, in the midst of dire straits, Jehoshaphat could have devised his own plan and asked God to bless it. Instead he proclaimed a fast, brought the people together to pray, reminded God of His promises to Abraham, and gave space for a prophetic word which ultimately was given through Jahaziel. In the morning he sent the choir out first before the warriors to meet the huge coalition of armies that had come against Judah. This was not a plan that any man would naturally dream up, but as we have seen, true worshiping musicians can accomplish so much in the spiritual realm that it confounds the enemy (2 Chron. 20). Through prayer, God's promises became reality.

How does God release the prophetic? Multiple avenues exist, and God utilizes many options and creative approaches, tailoring them to various circumstances and needs. After studying godly prophetic ministry and what is can look like, we will now turn our attention to considering the counterfeit.

Chapter Ten

False Prophets and False Apostles

"For false messiahs and false prophets will appear and perform great signs and wonders to deceive, if possible, even the elect. See, I have told you ahead of time."
Matthew 24:24

"For such people are false apostles, deceitful workers, masquerading as apostles of Christ."
2 Corinthians 11:13

Throughout the previous chapters we have studied the proper functioning of the apostolic and prophetic as seen throughout Scripture. Obviously both functions, when working as God intended, provide critical momentum, strength, energy, and life-giving ministry which the Church cannot afford to be without or to ignore.

Any pastor or church leader, however, has probably experienced at least one false prophet or false apostle. These can create havoc amongst the sheep. Indeed, they are sent from Satan to do precisely that. Confusion is not of the Lord (1 Cor. 14:33).

The Masquerade
In Matthew 24:10 Jesus is describing the end times and states this about the time just before He returns: "At that time many will turn away from the faith and will betray and hate each other, and many false prophets will appear and deceive many people." Here He

warns that there will be numerous false prophets, and lots of people will be deceived. The problem will certainly not be a small one. He goes on in Matthew 24:24 to restate that in the last days false messiahs and false prophets will come and through signs and wonders, they will try to deceive even Christians if they can. The devil surely likes to mess things up! Jesus follows this warning (v. 25) by stating, "See, I have told you ahead of time." We are not supposed to be shocked that these deceitful workers arise in the Church; He has already prophesied regarding it, warning us about them.

What is our reaction supposed to be to these false prophets, messiahs, and apostles? One temptation is to shut down all prophecy and other gifts of the Spirit in the church so that we do not get tricked. That should take care of it, right?

No, not at all. The problem with this approach is that it also shuts down the real work of the prophetic and apostolic. Since Ephesians 4:11 tells us that there are five gifts for the church (apostle, prophet, pastor, teacher, and evangelist), how could we not even accept two of the five gifts Jesus gave us? It effectively turns off two-fifths of the flow of the church. That is tragic almost beyond conception, and most certainly impacts the Church's effectiveness.

If the true and proper functioning of the apostolic and prophetic are either not working or are a trickle, then it gives space for Satan to step into that emptiness. This explains our situation today. The Church's understanding of these functions is so incomplete that we are apt to let in the false prophet and false apostle because most Christians aren't even clear what an authentic example looks like. It seems reasonable that the vacuum of the genuine in our end days is so great that it is opening the door for false prophets and apostles to take over and increase, just as Jesus prophesied (Matt. 24:11). We are actually causing the prophecy to come true!

We are warned not to extinguish the flames of the Spirit and not to hold prophecies in contempt.

We should not contribute to this void. Our antidote is to know what is real, be open to the move of the Spirit, and desire to hear what God wants to say and do in our church, the local community, and across the world. Certainly, this is the time to open up to valid apostolic and prophetic functioning as never before so we can counteract the false work of Satan.

In 1 Thessalonians 5:19-21 we are told: "Do not quench the Spirit. Do not treat prophecies with contempt but test them all; hold on to what is good, reject every kind of evil." This provides a clear directive. We are warned not to extinguish the flames of the Spirit and not to hold prophecies in contempt. Although it is tempting, when spurious prophecy occurs, to simply squelch all prophecy in the future, the clear mandate of Scripture is not to quench what the Spirit wants to do.

This warning is followed directly with another instruction: "but test them all." The same command is given in 1 John 4:1; "Dear friends, do not believe every spirit, but test the spirits to see whether they are from God, because many false prophets have gone out into the world."

What are the keys to testing prophecies and the spirits behind them? One way is to know Scripture and be certain that what is shared is in line with the Bible. We can also test them spiritually, by the fruit of the Spirit, by their humility and other personal traits. Additionally, we must understand what the authentic functions of the apostolic and prophetic look like so we can spot counterfeits.

Some verses in 2 Corinthians 11 shed even more light on this topic of false prophets and false apostles. Paul refers to "super-apostles" (v. 5) functioning at that time and giving him some trouble. Then in verses 13-15 he says, "For such people are false apostles, deceitful workers, masquerading as apostles of Christ. And no wonder, for Satan himself masquerades as an angel of light. It is not surprising, then, if his servants also masquerade as servants of righteousness. Their end will be what their actions deserve."

Satan likes to throw masquerade parties!

Satan likes to throw masquerade parties! Indeed, a major problem with false apostles and false prophets is that they are satanically placed and serve their evil leader, playing masquerade. Walter Martin, in his classic book *The Kingdom of the Cults*, said that "a biblical false prophet was a servant of the devil attempting to lead people away from the truth."[60] Think about this. They will act like an angel of light, putting on masks of righteousness, costumes that will make them appear to be something they are not. But who's behind that mask? Satan.

Jesus warned about this with a similar metaphor in Matthew 7:15: "Watch out for false prophets. They come to you in sheep's clothing, but inwardly they are ferocious wolves." This is another costume game. The wolves are dressing up like sheep. We cannot miss the point here that they are wolves, however—wolves that will masquerade their way into the fold and then devour the sheep. They therefore must be tested, recognized, and removed from the fold. This is the explicit responsibility of church leaders. An important part of the shepherd's job is taking care of the sheep. The sheep themselves can be taken unawares, but the shepherds should grow in their ability to recognize a masquerader.

Another set of instructive verses can be found in 2 Peter 2:1-3 (NASB):

> But false prophets also arose among the people, just as there will be false teachers among you, who will secretly bring in destructive heresies, even denying the Master who bought them, bringing upon themselves swift destruction. And many will follow their sensuality, and because of them the way of truth will be blasphemed. And in their greed they will exploit you with false words. Their condemnation from long ago is not idle, and their destruction is not asleep.

This provides even more description of the havoc that can be wreaked by false prophets and apostles as well as false teachers. The false roles bring in heresies which can destroy the church. These false teachers go so far as to deny Jesus (v. 1), but such disavowal can happen by not looking to Him, drawing attention to oneself instead of God, taking the credit rather than giving it to Him, or placing other things above Him. This is occurring now, and the warning that "many will follow their sensuality" (v. 2) is most sobering. The Word keeps warning that "many" are involved and here states that condemnation and destruction are "not idle or asleep." Sensuality has devastating effects.

"Sensuality" is appealing to our senses and our lusts. It may include a desire for certain entertainment, performance, and dazzling displays. This is not to say that media special effects, fog machines, videos, movement, and sound and lighting are automatically wrong; however, when the sole purpose is to draw attention to self and to please or fulfill the senses (the meaning of sensuality), it crosses a line. Because of sensuality, the true way to God will be diminished and even blasphemed, which basically indicates an irreverence towards God or sacred things.

> *When the sole purpose of special effects is to focus on self and please the senses, it crosses a line.*

These people will also be greedy, doing things for monetary gain, and as such, they exploit people for their own benefit. These are all clear signs that something is off. It is part of the "testing" we are required to do. Are they greedy, sensual, exploiting others? Beware! There is a vast difference between approaching ministry in a contemporary style and in crossing that fine line of biblical and scriptural holiness and reverence.

The above verses in 2 Peter 2 are preceded by some interesting verses in chapter 1:19-21:

> We also have the prophetic message as something completely reliable, and you will do well to pay attention to it, as to a light shining in a dark place, until the day dawns and the morning star rises in your hearts. Above all, you must understand that no prophecy of Scripture came about by the prophet's own interpretation of things. For prophecy never had its origin in the human will, but prophets, though human, spoke from God as they were carried along by the Holy Spirit.

These important contextual verses in 2 Peter 1 indicate that the genuine prophetic message is something completely reliable. We are instructed to pay attention as a "light shining in a dark place." This is in such contrast to the warning that follows in the next chapter, but the distinction is clear. No authentic prophecy comes about by the prophet's own thinking, their own ideas, or their interpretation of things. This is because the source of godly prophecy doesn't have its origin in human will. Rather the authentic prophetic voice speaks from God as the Holy Spirit carries them along. The Spirit instigates valid prophecy and moves through a person to share God's word. This is something we obviously would not ever want to reject.

In the next chapter and verse (2 Peter 2:1) there is that "But." "But false prophets also arose among the people." These did not have messages inspired by the Holy Spirit but instead ones that came from their own thinking or their friends or the culture rather than from God.

So, there are the authentic prophetic messages which are reliable and to which we should pay attention as to a light shining in a dark place, BUT false prophets also exist simultaneously. This leaves us with the great need to test the spirits and increase in our level of discernment.

Thornbushes and Thistles

In the last section we quoted the verse from Matthew 7:15, "Watch out for false prophets. They come to you in sheep's clothing, but inwardly they are ferocious wolves." The next verse then provides an excellent way of testing a person's spirit: "By their fruit you will recognize them. Are grapes gathered from thornbushes, or figs from thistles?"

Good fruit doesn't come out of a prickly, bristly, thorny attitude.

We can remove someone's mask by looking at their heart which reveals itself in specific behavior. People who are sincerely Christians will be known by the fruit of the Spirit. But those unattached to Jesus Christ, the vine, will be unable to produce the fruit of the Spirit consistently on their own since the Holy Spirit is the one who works in the individual to produce the fruit. They don't get real fruit simply by their own will, and ultimately, they will show they are made of plastic if they are trying to deceive others. Good fruit like figs and grapes don't grow out of thornbushes or thistles. Those are both so prickly. If we are dealing with someone who is "prickly," i.e., contrary, difficult to work with, bristly, barbed, and thorny, we can be sure they are false prophets or apostles or teachers. Watch out! Don't get scratched! They are poisonous. Jesus told us here exactly how to discover the wolves in sheep's clothing and end the masquerade.

What does Galatians 5:19-23 show us regarding the fruit of the Spirit and the opposite—acts of the flesh?

> The acts of the flesh are obvious: sexual immorality, impurity and debauchery, idolatry and witchcraft; hatred, discord, jealousy, fits of rage, selfish ambition, dissensions, factions and envy; drunkenness, orgies, and the like. I warn you, as I did before, that those who live like this will not inherit the kingdom of God. But the fruit of the Spirit is love, joy, peace, forbearance, kindness, goodness, faithfulness, gentleness and self-control.

A false worker in any of the five-fold giftings will exhibit acts of the flesh. Notice the high number of these which have to do with relationships: discord, jealousy, hatred, dissensions, factions, fits of rage, envy, and even the sexual problems named. When people are working in the prophetic, apostolic, or teaching categories but are leaving strained relationships in their wake, they fit into the false category.

The fruit of the spirit, though, includes traits which bring about nice, pleasant relationships; love, gentleness, patience, peace, kindness, and self-control. Such people will be faithful and responsible, full of good things and great attitudes. They are "sweet fruit." The apostles were peaceful, long-suffering leaders. As for the biblical prophets, they knew God's care for His children was not some kind of nebulous theory. They recognized His love and exhibited it in specific ways that were direct and clear cut. Demonstrating patience and self-control, faithfulness and goodness, the biblical apostles and prophets offered hope based on God's abiding presence and personal care for the Jewish people.

Authentic workers will consistently exhibit the fruit of the Spirit.

Consequences ensued for a prophet who did not exhibit the fruit of the Spirit— even a faithful one such as Moses when he became impatient and angry and struck the rock (Num. 20:11). Moses was not allowed to take the people into the Promised Land. For rightful workers in the apostolic and prophetic, the fruit of the Spirit must be consistently exhibited.

Because of the import of these traits, leaders today should get to know the people who are allowed to minister publicly, being certain they have the fruit of the Spirit. As most seasoned in the ministry already realize (sometimes after a negative experience), we don't lightly hand over a microphone to someone we don't know. We are careful to test the spirit first, becoming acquainted and observing what this person is like over a period of time.

If we don't know the person, often we have a strong sense of discernment from the Lord whether an individual is acting in accordance with the Spirit or not. Of course, we can still be duped by the masquerade game, but discernment grows with time in the ministry.

I (Carolyn) remember two distinct occasions when I was visiting a church where the pastor did not know me, but he handed me the microphone to give a word. I believe there was an inner witness, and he recognized that I was safe, perhaps because I had waited for the right moment and gone to him personally to seek guidance as to what I should do with that word.

Likewise, I have sensed that something is really off. I remember once when we were wanting to hire someone. A number of people interviewed him and liked him, ultimately recommending the hire. He had good experience and background; there was not a single reason we shouldn't offer him the job—except for him. I had a "check in my Spirit." When it came down to the decision, the other individual making the final decision with me learned of this "check" and said, "We're not hiring him."

I said, "But I have nothing to go on but this feeling."

He retorted, "Yes, and that is enough. I call it my 'knower.' And every single time I have not listened to my knower, I have been sorry." We didn't hire him, and a few weeks after he would have been in his position with us, we learned of a large moral failure. It would have had severe ramifications within our ministry if we hadn't listened to what I believe was God's discerning check from the Spirit. We must recognize the importance of the spiritual gift of "distinguishing between spirits" (I Cor. 12:10) and be open to its ministry.

Many have probably witnessed people who have used the prophetic gifting as a demand that they need to be heard or given a platform, but they have a sort of razor edge. If they are sharing a "word" that is demeaning and abrasive, this is not of the Lord. They may indicate they just see things as they are and so that explains why they are "in your face." If the "prophet" delights in being rude and harsh and tells people off, we've got a problem on our hands.

Additionally, if a leader addresses this attitude but the giver of the prophecy is haughty regarding the correction and exhibits a very bad attitude, they are showing what is actually in the heart. That sort of behavior does not match up with the fruit of the Spirit and should be addressed. They should be confronted one-on-one and then handled with the elders/deacons and told to leave the church if the rebellious attitude still continues.

Guiding and Developing the Apostolic/Prophetic Flow

Proper prophetic and apostolic work demands that any correction be carried out with sobriety, loving care, and a sense of pain rather than haughty aggression. Humility oozes from genuine prophetic or apostolic workers, both in delivering and receiving correction. They do not get touchy or snappy when other church leaders question them. In fact, they are open to discuss their experiences and situations because they are eager to do things well and are desirous for growth. They view personal guidance for themselves as helpful because they want the ministry to be pure and proper. Still, things are not always perfect when we deal with people. Misunderstandings and the need for learning, development, and maturation can come from many angles.

One area we need to commit to as church leaders is to be patient while people grow. We should remember that some people attempt to move in the Spirit before they have become mature in personality or in spirituality. These may not have acquired enough fruit of the Spirit to respond well to correction, but this does not automatically mean they fall into the false category. We should be patient with those who may be defensive or immature, not writing them off from future ministry, but rather coming alongside to help them learn and grow in the work of the Spirit. If, however, the prophetic and apostolic workers are unwilling to undergo any developmental assistance, they may have to be stopped if they are in error. When we confront gently, however, such a difficult move might be averted.

The attitude of church leaders should be one of guiding, teaching, and fostering.

In other situations, some leaders do not themselves fully grasp the prophetic or apostolic and may try to correct inappropriately. They should learn all they can about proper, biblical functioning so they do not demean authentic work. There is never a reason to make fun of the prophetic or any of the five-fold ministries.

Still other problems may come from congregants who do not grasp the work of the gifts. Just because someone was offended at a word or action carried out by a prophetic or apostolic worker does not automatically mean that word was wrong. Sometimes it is the complainer who needs to receive more explanation and instruction.

The attitude of church leaders overall should be one of guiding, teaching, and fostering appropriate apostolicity and prophetic ministry in our midst. Budding workers in these areas are sometimes unsure of how to proceed but are trying to be obedient to what God is saying to them. They may make some innocent mistakes because they don't know exactly how these gifts are supposed to function. Such people will benefit from encouragement and gentle teaching. Tender shoots can be easily squashed. Unfortunately, I (Carolyn) have seen some hurt and trampled little "budding plants" so confused about what they should do next. They have clammed up and backed off, but with teaching, explanation, and proper modeling, they begin to thrive for the Kingdom.

Robert Greenleaf made a meaningful observation about this:

> The variable that marks some periods as barren and some as rich in prophetic vision is in the interest, the level of seeking, the responsiveness of the hearers. The variable is *not* in the presence or absence or the relative quality and force of the prophetic voices. The prophet grows in stature as people respond to his message. If his early attempts are ignored or spurned, his talent may wither away. It is *seekers,* then, who make the prophet; and the initiative of any one of us in searching for and responding to the voice of the contemporary prophet may mark the turning point in his or her growth and service.[61]

In order to strengthen these God-given ministries in the church, seasoned leaders should be open to who God wants to call forth and anoint. This includes observing peoples' spiritual growth and fruit, a sure sign that God's Spirit is at work. Jesus, Paul, Moses and so many other biblical leaders noticed potential and built a team whom they mentored for some time. They worked together for a while, with the mentors observing and testing the fruit, character, spiritual maturity, mettle, faithfulness, and wisdom of their new protégés. When ready, the mentees were sent out to other places to do their own ministry. These leaders were not jealous of those on their team. They wanted them to thrive and do well.

When Moses' seventy elders were chosen, Numbers 11:24-29 tells us that God "took some of the power of the Spirit that was on him and put it on the seventy." Then "[w]hen the Spirit rested on them, they prophesied...." Whenever the Spirit of God rests on any of us, mentors and mentees alike, there is a flow of the prophetic and other gifts of the Spirit. There were even two elders who "remained in the camp" who began to prophesy, and a young man ran and told Moses. Joshua spoke up and asked Moses to stop them from prophesying. However, Moses made an interesting reply: "Are you jealous for my sake? I wish that all the Lord's people were prophets and that the Lord would put his Spirit on them!"

Every church leader should desire to see all the gifts flow freely and for the Spirit to genuinely come upon anybody and everybody dedicated to God. The biblical prophets wanted to share what they had and were led by God to anoint others as kings or prophets. These included Samuel anointing both Saul and David, and Elijah anointing two kings as well as his prophetic successor, Elisha. Our model Jesus prayed and chose disciples to accompany him. Upon these twelve, the future church would be established. First, however, they needed to be tapped out and developed, and Jesus gave the rest of His life to this task. Paul assembled a team which he mentored and sent out. Among these were Timothy whose role as an evangelist Paul noted and commissioned. Leaders very often sense God's calling upon somebody else and choose to share the limelight and guide them, pointing out what potential they see.

Wendy, one of my (Carolyn's) friends, recently told me the story of her husband Del being called into pastoral ministry. He clearly recognized that God was asking him to move into the pastorate, but she was resistant, not wanting to be a pastor's wife. One day they went to a luncheon where Mike, a stranger from England who functioned in the prophetic, was the speaker. As Mike was talking, he pointed to Wendy's husband and said, "You are a pastor who..." and went on speaking. Del interrupted, saying he was not a pastor. And Mike quipped, "Well, you are called to be, and you will have many years of effective ministry." This confirmed to my friend that Del was indeed appointed by God and from then on, Wendy had no question about her calling either. He later passed away, but she herself has since been a church planter and lead pastor. The prophetic confirmation is what cinched it for her, though. We need the flow of the prophetic so validation can come regarding God's call to the ministry.

Recognition and encouragement of the next generation leaders in their five-fold gifting brings purpose and provides an important covering. It gives a level of assurance and strength. Literal anointing is only a symbol of what God is already doing in the heart and life of the person. If we want more authentic apostolic and prophetic workers, we must find them and help them grow and develop instead of leaving them in confusion about how to proceed. This takes time and conscious effort, but the results are well worth it.

Handling False Prophets and False Apostles in the Church

False prophets and false apostles who do not have the fruit of the Spirit but rather the deeds of the flesh cannot be left to create problems in the church. They can cause church splits, dissensions, and factions, teach false doctrine, and totally mess up and even defile everything they touch. They need to be identified and removed.

At the end of Paul's second letter to the Corinthians he describes in chapters 11, 12, and 13 a group of "super-apostles" (11:5). A summarization of highlights from these three chapters indicates that they were creating some real problems. It seems they preached a different Jesus and a different gospel. They were exuding a different spirit than the Spirit of God. Apparently, they were slick speakers and expected to be paid, which Paul did not at all expect for himself. Theses imposters were presenting themselves as being important, putting on airs, boasting, taking advantage of the Corinthians, and exploiting them. Notice again the lack of the fruit of the Spirit, but instead the prevalence of the "acts of the flesh."

Paul explained that he didn't want to be defensive (12:19), but he had some things to boast about too, and these things end up being the opposite of the super-apostles. He shared "his resumé" of what we have noted as the mark of a genuine apostle: suffering, paying a price, not ministering for personal gain. Paul then talked about being an apostle out of his weaknesses so God could be strong in him. He bemoaned that when he came, he was afraid "that there may be discord, jealousy, fits of rage, selfish ambition, slander, gossip, arrogance and disorder. I am afraid that when I come again my God will humble me before you, and I will be grieved over many who have sinned earlier and have not repented of the impurity, sexual sin and debauchery in which they have indulged" (2 Cor. 12:20b-21).

Paul went on to state that he would take care of these problems when he arrived. This is his apostolicity speaking. He is required to keep the DNA of the church doctrine, maintain the purity of the church, and not allow sin to infest the church. He says in 2 Corinthians 13:2b-4:

> On my return I will not spare those who sinned earlier or any of the others, since you are demanding proof that Christ is speaking through me. He is not weak in dealing with you, but is powerful among you. For to be sure, he was crucified in weakness, yet he lives by God's power. Likewise, we are weak in him, yet by God's power we will live with him in our dealing with you.

Those definitely called to the prophetic and apostolicity cannot spare the confrontation of sin in the Church. Christ Himself is strong in dealing with sin within the church. This shows us what church leaders must do to handle any false apostles and prophets, false teachers and others who are habitually acting out of the flesh and creating problems within the body of Christ.

> *Don't' let the wolf devour the sheep. Unmask Satan. Something must be done.*

Don't let the wolf devour the sheep. Get the bad apple out of the barrel before it makes other apples around it rotten. Unmask Satan. Don't play the game of masquerade. God's power will help church leaders in their weakness, but something must be done. Don't cower, but rather be strong in the Lord.

One way of determining how deep the "falseness" actually goes is to have a personal talk and see how the person responds to godly guidance. A female pastoral colleague of mine (Carolyn) called for my advice one night. The church leadership was dealing with a gal who had a rather prickly attitude. She seemed haughty at times and potentially divisive. She thought of herself as a prophet and felt her attitude was justified because of her prophetic bent. The question was this: Was this lady simply untrained and untutored, or was she a hazard to the flock? We came up with a plan. Ask her to come in to chat. Offer to meet with her in the future to discuss the prophetic and its proper working. Would she have a teachable spirit? If so, perhaps she could learn and grow. She came in once but refused the offer of ongoing mentoring. In just several weeks, she left the church.

Encourage the true. Do not quench the Spirit. Mentor and train up the next generation of apostolic and prophetic workers who evidence much fruit in their lives. For those who are false, handle the wolf!

Chapter Eleven

Building Discernment

"Discernment is not a matter of simply telling the difference between right and wrong; rather it is telling the difference between right and almost right."[62]
Charles Spurgeon

Since false prophets and false apostles clearly are slick and deceptive, it is highly important to keep growing in discernment. Rather than shut down genuine functioning in either of these areas, the onus is upon church leaders to cultivate their spiritual ability and wisdom to discern and handle situations which are not from God.

Spurgeon pointed out that discernment is not just knowing the distinction between obvious right and wrong. Rather it is knowing the difference between right and almost right. When somebody is almost right, but not entirely, the question—as we have already alluded—is whether they are masking serious issues or whether they basically have a good heart and can be helped and guided.

The 21 Item Checklist: What Makes Something "Off"?
In discerning whether something is off or not, let's create a checklist that summarizes various points to consider. In looking at those working in the apostolic or prophetic ministry, we need to discern the following:

1. Are they scriptural, **OR** does what they preach and teach not line up with the Bible?
2. Do they confess and point to Jesus, **OR** do they take the emphasis off Him and highlight other things instead of His death and resurrection for forgiveness of sins?
3. Are their prayer lives apparent and robust, **OR** do they not care about the prayer meetings or their own time with God because they are just "too busy" with other "important" work?
4. Do they evidence the fruit of the Spirit **OR** the sins of the flesh? Are they prickly? What readily oozes out of them behind stage or in stressful situations or when they don't get their way?
5. Do they live holy lives, **OR** are they toying with various immoral behaviors or questionable ethics? Is their speech unclean; do they tell off-color jokes?
6. Are they humble, preferring others above themselves, **OR** are they prideful, drawing attention to themselves and wanting always to occupy center stage?
7. Do they desire and seek out appropriate covering and accountability, **OR** do they spurn such, preferring instead to bring around them their own friends who are unlikely to confront them? Do they go to others like Paul did going to Jerusalem to submit his revelation or do they function independently?
8. Do they work within the church structure, **OR** do they spurn the working of the local churches and try to set up their own little empire outside of the church, drawing sheep away from their local fold?
9. Do they not seek monetary gain, **OR** are they out to see how much they can be paid or pull in by marketing their wares?
10. Are they willing to suffer for Christ's sake and pay the price that comes with their calling, **OR** are they looking for ease and fame?
11. When they have a tough message to give from God, do they share this with pain and the fear of the Lord **OR** with haughtiness and a judgmental spirit, evidencing a self-righteous attitude?
12. Are they willing to deal with the spiritual push-back that

will occur when they move into Satan's territory, **OR** do they run when "all hell breaks loose"?
13. Do they move in signs and wonders which give all the glory to God **OR** instead in signs and wonders generated by the enemy to deceive others, ones which bring attention to the false prophets and apostles and the "great" things they can do?
14. Do they want to move toward unity, being peacemakers and drawing people together, **OR** are they divisive and leave factions in their wake?
15. Are they no respecter of persons, clearly loving everybody no matter their race, culture, gender, looks, health, or financial status, **OR** do they try to get into the graces of the "right folks"?
16. Through the grace of God do they move in the gifts of the Spirit and follow His leading, **OR** are they not sensitive to the Holy Spirit and His direction, desiring to be in personal control?
17. Are they teachable and open to correction, guidance, and growth in their ministry, **OR** are they "above" any of these things, acting as if they really don't need anybody else telling them anything?
18. Are they full of integrity, transparent, and humanly "real," **OR** are they masquerading, hiding their inner selves, full of deceit?
19. Do they honor people, complementing the other roles in the five-fold ministry and allowing them to shine in what they have been called to do, **OR** do they demean other ministers or try to eclipse them?
20. Are they real servants to others **OR** do they expect to be served and honored by others?
21. Do they speak and do what God would have them do no matter what, **OR** do they make decisions independently of God's direction, appealing to itching ears and telling people what they want to hear?

False Prophets and False Apostles Fill In the Void
When a vacuum of real apostolic and prophetic functioning is allowed to exist, the Church feels it and so does society. The thought of an apostolic and prophetic void in our world today brings to mind

some famous words of a song probably most will recognize:

> "Fools," I said, "you do not know
> Silence like a cancer grows
> Hear my words that I might teach you,
> Take my arms that I might reach you"
> But my words like silent raindrops fell,
> And echoed
> In the wells of silence
> And the people bowed and prayed
> To the neon God they made
> And the sign flashed its warning,
> In the words that it was forming
> And the sign said, "The words of the prophets
> Are written on the subway walls
> And tenement halls
> And whispered in the sounds of silence."[63]

Paul Simon recognized that prophetic words, when they are not spoken, create a silence that grows like a cancer, even resulting in the neon gods of idolatry. In this voiceless emptiness, people cannot hear what God is saying. They cannot dwell in His well of Truth. Their only hope is to take human "wisdom" and man-made "prophecy" off the graffiti walls. This has happened in our society today. People are reading and believing garbage.

What exactly happens, then, when apostolic and prophetic ministries are not operating properly? The outcomes are alarming. First of all, human flesh tries to fill in the gap. A.W. Tozer said, "This frightening hour calls aloud for men in the gift of prophetic insight. Instead we have men who conduct surveys, polls and panel discussions."[64] Instead of listening to God and moving under His power and direction, today we tend to replace that with our own man-made approaches.

When godly functioning in the apostolic/prophetic fails to occur, Satan fills in with a substitute.

Then when true godly functioning fails to occur, Satan is more than happy to substitute. His minions take over as false prophets and false apostles. Just like these false roles exhibited themselves within the Jewish milieu, so they delight in taking up residence within the Church. These bogus usurpers will create as much havoc as possible. As just delineated, the various negative actions and attitudes on the other side of the OR kicks in and takes up residence. This results in divisions, hurt people, confusion, deceit, and pretending. If this sounds serious, it is.

When there are no positive and healthy models of apostolic and prophetic functioning, then what is left are problematic, warped paradigms at best and completely false examples spawned by Satan at worst. Right now, if one googles "prophetic" or "apostolic," there is little good teaching that pops up. What does especially proliferate in such a search are numerous Mormon sites and even Muslim ones who proclaim their own prophets, including Muhammad himself who was designated as a prophet to present and confirm monotheistic teachings.

Even in our everyday contemporary society, all sorts of personae are acting like "prophets." They are speaking out, correcting others, saying what they think will happen, giving warnings, and basically choosing to idolize their own opinions without so much as an iota of thought about what God Himself might think about any of it. Such egocentrism, plus devilish counterfeiting, creates far more problems than if the Church allowed Jesus' apostolic and prophetic gifts to function fully. Sure, even among God-fearing people, there are still situations that need to be corrected, but since we trust the Spirit, it is far better to let Him pour out the gifts in our midst than it is to shut His Spirit down or out. We must go back to the way Jesus intended for His church to be established, operate, and grow.

To allow for such a flow of God's Spirit, the first step is to know and understand the great breadth of function God intended for the apostolic and prophetic. This book was designed to build and expand these concepts into the everyday life of the church. We must become more astute in recognizing and naming valid apostolic and prophetic functioning in our midst. We can identify proper working with such observations as "That was a great example of proper prophetic functioning at work" or "You just heard from a godly person serving apostolically." We can point out what makes it authentic. This way people can begin to learn for themselves how to discern and not get deceived by the false.

Right now, the Church struggles to identify godly apostolic and prophetic workers. If asked to name five pastors, five evangelists, and five Bible teachers, average church people could probably do so. However, ask them to name five people who are serving apostolically and five functioning prophetically, and they would probably struggle. Part of this is due to undeveloped concepts of what these roles entail. If instructed to include missionaries in the apostolic thinking, most would go "Ah!" and come up with five names. Still, we might find them naming missionaries whether or not they were educators (teachers), pastoring, or serving as evangelists. The prophetic? It's doubtful they could name one, except perhaps somebody who is often used in the verbal gifts of prophecy in the church service. But the broader, fuller perspective of the prophetic? No, probably not. Still, whether anybody else can identify them or not, so many are humbly serving God in these capacities in out-of-the-way places and in their prayer rooms and meetings.

> *Right now, the Church struggles to identify godly apostolic and prophetic workers.*

What are the developmental differences between these humble God-servants and those who are false prophets and apostles? Everybody—whether they ultimately choose to bend the knee to God or not—is given certain personality traits and personal giftings at birth which are designed to glorify the Lord. Some would be called into a five-fold role of some sort if they became Christians. Jeremiah, for example, was strategically designed from conception to be a prophet: "Before I formed you in the womb I knew you, before you were born I set you apart; I appointed you as a prophet to the nations" (Jer. 1:4-5).

If people do not come to know God, however, then those natural giftings may be perverted to the dark side. This explains how the fortune tellers and psychics work their wares. They have natural giftings and when accompanied by demonic insight and foresight (which is partial because they are not omniscient like God), they can function correctly enough of the time that people will spend money to have their palms read or their fortunes told.

Prophetic messages that are genuinely from God, however, are never wrong. Take a moment to read carefully Deuteronomy 18:14-22 since it contains some critical information:

> The nations you will dispossess listen to those who practice sorcery or

Building Discernment

divination. But as for you, the Lord your God has not permitted you to do so. The Lord your God will raise up for you a prophet like me [Moses] from among you, from your fellow Israelites. You must listen to him. For this is what you asked of the Lord your God at Horeb on the day of the assembly when you said, "Let us not hear the voice of the Lord our God nor see this great fire anymore, or we will die." The Lord said to me: "What they say is good. I will raise up for them a prophet like you from among their fellow Israelites, and I will put my words in his mouth. He will tell them everything I command him. I myself will call to account anyone who does not listen to my words that the prophet speaks in my name. But a prophet who presumes to speak in my name anything I have not commanded, or a prophet who speaks in the name of other gods, is to be put to death." You may say to yourselves, "How can we know when a message has not been spoken by the Lord?" If what a prophet proclaims in the name of the Lord does not take place or come true, that is a message the Lord has not spoken. That prophet has spoken presumptuously, so do not be alarmed.

This shows us a number of points that are critical to this discussion: 1) God does not want anybody seeking fortune tellers or psychics. He has appointed genuine prophets. 2) God raised up prophets when the Israelites said they did not want to hear God's voice any more. 3) The Lord said it was good to have prophets, that He would raise them up, and that He would put His own words in their mouths. 4) The Lord declared the prophets would say everything God commanded them to say. 5) God Himself would call to account anyone who didn't listen to God's words given by a prophet who speaks in the Lord's name (a rightful prophet). 6) How do we test if a prophecy is correct or not? Well, a proper prophecy will ultimately come to pass. If the prophecy doesn't occur, then the prophet has spoken presumptuously, and we are not to be alarmed.

Prophetic messages that are genuinely from God are never wrong.

Deuteronomy 13:1-5 states some similar ideas: If a prophet tries to lead people to "follow other gods" (v. 2), the people should not listen to that prophet. Then verse 5 says, "That prophet or dreamer must be put to death for inciting rebellion against the Lord your God, who brought you out of Egypt and redeemed you from the land of slavery. That prophet or dreamer tried to turn you from the way the Lord your God commanded you to follow. You must purge the evil from among you."

We see, then, that giving false prophecy which incited rebellion against God was serious enough to demand the death penalty. Shall we therefore murder someone whose prophecy does not come to pass? No, of course not. Human error can come in with even the most well-meaning people who love the Lord with all of their hearts. However, if the person is a false prophet sowing many false prophecies which do not come to pass and also inciting rebellion against God, they must be handled and removed ("purged") from the sheepfold.

When it comes to fortune tellers and other diviners, the world is spending a great deal of money on making calls to psychics, going to palm readers and fortune tellers, and believing in crystal balls, tarot cards, and horoscopes. The real prophetic flow out of the Church ought to be even more robust, drawing people to Almighty God and right living and demonstrating His power and grace in their lives. God help us to place the prophetic function back into the Church with the strength that God has intended all along. We who are Pentecostal and say we value the things of the Spirit ought to have a full stream of ever emerging true prophecy that issues forth—not only into the Church but into society—bringing truth, correction, confirmation, and encouragement wherever it goes. God help us to make this a reality as God intended.

When Jesus gave His five gifts to the Church, He planned for all five to be in operation. We would shudder to remove evangelism. We cannot imagine the churches without pastors and teachers to care for and disciple new converts and the whole congregation. But in some places the church is ingrown and is not reaching out into the community and the world. The apostolic flow is not what it could be. In even more places the prophetic is not functioning at all.

We need to be as aghast that these two important streams are not surging forth as we would if any of the other three streams halted. We are missing as much as if we took away evangelism or pastors or teachers. Perhaps we are lacking even more since we are told in Ephesians 2:19-20 that as "members of his household" we are being "built on the foundation of the apostles and prophets, with Jesus Christ himself as the chief cornerstone." We definitely can't do without a cornerstone, and we know the results of building with a presently shifting foundation.

False Prophets and False Apostles Take the Easy Way Out
Another way of identifying false workers is that they are unwilling to suffer. Those who were honored in Scripture were false prophets and false apostles. The authentic ones were thrown into prison, threatened, flogged, left for dead, killed by the sword, and driven into the desert; they were destitute, persecuted, and mistreated (Hebrews 11:35b-38—Note that v. 32 indicates they were referring to prophets, et al.).

In Christopher Hitchens's Foreword to Aldous Huxley's *Brave New World*, Hitchens said, "We can always be sure of one thing—that the messengers of discomfort and sacrifice will be stoned and pelted by those who wish to preserve at all costs their own contentment. This is not a lesson that is confined to the Testaments."[65]

In some scriptural stories the hearer(s) of a confronting word from God were able to move out of their contentment and repent—like when the prophet Jonah faced his Assyrian arch-enemy with their sin (Jonah 1:1-3; 3:1-10). That entire culture had to shift, and this could not have been an easy thing! However, all too often people do not want to change; they like their sin. A common response to any challenge from God is often to persecute the bearer of the word—the prophet.

Both 1 and 2 Kings might actually be titled "1 and 2 Kings v. Prophets." In the long run it was God's prophetic word that determined Israel's history and even drove the storylines in these two books. Narratives abound of kings who did not listen to the prophets and faced tragic consequences. The words of the Lord made them angry. In their rebellion they did not heed the warnings, often taking out their frustration on the prophet. An example is recorded in Jeremiah 38 where the prophet was thrown down into a cistern and left there in the waterless, muddy hole. Jeremiah had dispatched the truthful but discouraging message God required of him, and King Zedekiah had refused to listen. Still, God's word through the prophet came to pass.

Those truly called to prophetic and apostolic work will be able to understand the spiritual dynamics of what is happening when they obey God. The Lord will enable them to stand strong in the midst of persecution, misunderstanding, and repercussions. One of my (Carolyn's) favorite little biblical insights is tucked away in Revelation 22:6 where it says in the original Greek, "the Lord, the God of the spirits of the prophets," and then it goes on. This has always spoken to me of the fact that God Himself is watching over the very spirits of the prophets. He keeps them safe in His hand, and He will help them in their prophetic tasks, even though these can sometimes be trying. There is so much security when God is guiding, guarding, and keeping the prophetic spirit itself!

The Lord is "the God of the spirits of the prophets."

Those who are false prophets and apostles will not put up with difficulties. They will run or compromise, unwilling to pay a price. Jesus gave instructions on how to react in the midst of trouble. He said, "Blessed are you when people insult you, persecute you and falsely say all kinds of evil against you because of me. Rejoice and be glad, because great is your reward in heaven, for in the same way they persecuted the prophets who were before you" (Matt. 5:11-12).

Those serving God will take persecution with the deep joy and the strength of the Lord rather than with dejection and fear. It will not always be easy to get to that place of joy, but they will get there. They will see the challenges as part and parcel of their calling and will not skirt what they are asked to do just so they can escape troubles. Instead of seeking ease, they are willing to die to themselves and pick up their cross daily. This is an important litmus test in revealing those definitely called and those who are not; it is a dividing line between false and true apostles and prophets. Authentic workers will go to any extent to serve God and others, and they will not act like a martyr about it either.

Considering the slew of challenges faced by authentic prophetic or apostolic individuals, it would be tragic if they also had to endure abandonment from other Christian leaders. If we are to increase the flow of the prophetic and apostolic, there needs to be a greater level of identification, understanding, support, guidance, and appreciation for true servants of God who are following close after Jesus. They should not be left to fend for themselves in isolation from other church leadership.

Focusing on Function Rather Than Title Is Crucial

Titles often seem to be very important to false prophets and apostles. However, actually functioning in the five-fold gifts is far more important than any title or notoriety. Ephesians 4:11-13 indicates that all five gifts are still meant to function:

> So Christ himself gave the apostles, the prophets, the evangelists, the pastors and teachers, to equip his people for works of service, so that the body of Christ may be built up until we all reach unity in the faith and in the knowledge of the Son of God and become mature, attaining to the whole measure of the fullness of Christ.

Jesus Himself gave us these five gifts to utilize so the body of Christ could be built up and strengthened, and we are told this is to continue "until" we all reach unity, knowledge of Jesus, and maturity. In fact, we are to grow so very mature that we become like Jesus, attaining to the whole measure (not just a part) of the fullness of Christ Himself.

Probably few would argue that we have not yet reached this goal. We have much more maturity to gain, and a lot more work to do. The Church has not yet reached its maximum wholeness to the point where we could take a break. We still have many souls who need to be saved and discipled, and there are yet unreached people in a multitude of places where churches should be planted. So many groups, both and in and outside our own country, are far from being saturated with the gospel message. These include the deaf, various immigrant groups, rural communities where drugs are running rampant, and the list goes on. All of this indicates a deep need for apostolic functioning.

Joel prophesied that God would pour out His Spirit on all flesh, pointing out the Father's desire for the prophetic, dreams, and visions (Joel 2:28-29). Peter refers to this very verse on the day of Pentecost, explaining the outpouring of the Spirit upon those who had gathered for the feast of Shavuot. Remember that dreams and visions are part of the prophetic, and here they are emphasized to indicate the fullness of the prophetic.

Pentecostals believe that the Holy Spirit was poured out at Pentecost and continues into this day. As Christians open up to the Spirit, He gives abundantly to all people, the old and the young, the men and the women. God expects the prophetic and apostolic to continue in a strong release as on the Day of Pentecost when Peter's prophetic sermon resulted in thousands coming to the Lord. This continued through the great apostolic thrusts that established the Church across vast territory.

> *God expects the prophetic and apostolic to continue in a strong release as on the Day of Pentecost.*

Commitment to the idea of God's Spirit being poured out on "all flesh" is critical to a proper understanding of what He wants to accomplish in our society today. We need even more in our churches who are trained in the prophetic and apostolic—who can do their part, as called by God, to move in the Spirit, not just inside the church but outside of it as well. Desire for these ministries needs to couple with God's leading and empowerment so the Spirit shakes our culture to the core. On the day of Pentecost, after Peter had preached to a crowd from many cultures, "they were cut to the heart and said to Peter and the other apostles, 'Brothers, what shall we do?' Peter replied, 'Repent and be baptized, every one of you, in the name of Jesus Christ for the forgiveness of your sins. And you will receive the gift of the Holy Spirit'" (Acts 2:37-38). Our message still must be that Jesus saves and the Holy Spirit continues to work.

More people need to be open to moving in all the gifts of the Spirit, including the prophetic and apostolic. God works through the Church body as a whole. Apostolicity and prophetic ministry are both designed to emerge in various places and numerous forms throughout the churches, functioning as a normal part of our everyday lives. Clearly their flow is meant to be vast and not limited to just a few "super-leaders."

The authors have chosen not to utilize the titles "prophets" and "apostles" for these functions in the modern-day Church. Although we would be careful not to assume automatically that anyone using a title is a false prophet or apostle, we are not comfortable espousing the general use of these two titles today. Some groups have been more culturally prone to assume the terms, and fine people are serving in meaningful Kingdom capacities. After all, no one thinks it odd to call an individual a pastor, a teacher, or an evangelist, but often to call someone an apostle or prophet in today's context is awkward and even objectionable. Why is that?

One reason is that some are assuming these titles and self-designed roles in grandiose ways which seem suspect to many. Few people care for the approach of such individuals out to make a name for themselves or wanting to be venerated in some special way. This kind of talk is not needed: "Oh, have you heard apostle so and so speak? Let's fly to see him! There's a big convention." or "Have you read the latest prophecy from....?" The following kind of comment is much more vital: "Oh, we have to pray that the Lord will show us how best to interact with that new group of Hmong who just moved in to our community. How can our church welcome them and show God's love?" We can never forget this: The actual functioning is far more important than a mere title.

A Biblical Look at Titles

Many are quietly functioning in the apostolic and prophetic without titles. They are the unsung heroes around the globe. Vinson Synan's thinking about this is worth considering:

> The nearest parallel to the New Testament and historic use of the term of apostle are those missionaries—often unnamed, untouted—who are bringing the message of the gospel for the first time to previously unreached peoples and tribes. They are busy translating Scripture and planting new churches where none exist. They have little time to consider their apostolic office.
>
> It is axiomatic to say that anyone who claims to be an apostle probably is *not* one. An apostle is not self-appointed or elected by any ecclesiastical body, but is chosen by the Lord Himself. As Lewi Pethrus, founder of the famous Filadelphia Church in Stockholm, Sweden, has said, anyone who claims apostleship is suspect. The one most likely to be an apostle is he who, like John the Baptist, claims only to be "a voice crying in the wilderness."
>
> Who are the apostles today? Perhaps we are asking the wrong question. Where do we find apostolic ministry—and apostolic results? These are what the modern church needs—far more than names to carry as a title or warm bodies to fill an office.[66]

John the Baptist kept being asked who he was (John 1), but he provided a simplistic answer: "A voice crying." He refused all other titles or identifications. Always humble, John was willing to decrease (John 3:30) in order to carry out his prophetic work of preparing the way for Jesus. The results were what mattered to him. This attitude carries over to true apostolic and prophetic workers.

They are always willing to decrease, while those who are false, on the other hand, are wanting their increase.

> **Authentic workers are willing to decrease, while false ones are wanting their increase.**

Scripture indicates that the Trinity deserves the major focus, not any human effort. God is really the One accomplishing the apostolic and prophetic work: initiating it, guiding it, and empowering it. Titles can open the door to pride and then lead on to deception. When God is at work, we bow down because He deserves the glory!

Jesus Himself was not quick to appreciate titles. In fact, in Matthew 23:8-12 He cautioned His disciples to be leery about their use:

> "But you are not to be called 'Rabbi,' for you have one Teacher, and you are all brothers. And do not call anyone on earth 'father,' for you have one Father, and he is in heaven. Nor are you to be called instructors, for you have one Instructor, the Messiah. The greatest among you will be your servant. For those who exalt themselves will be humbled, and those who humble themselves will be exalted."

Though the terms "apostle" and "prophet" were used often in both the Old and New Testaments, even then the titles carried some concern. In Revelation 2:2 Jesus complimented the church at Ephesus because they "tested those who claim to be apostles but are not, and have found them false" (Rev. 2:2). Even in those days, people were wrongly assuming the title of "apostle" for themselves or else had that title incorrectly bestowed upon them by others.

Jesus warned about a wrong attitude in Matthew 20:25-28:

> You know that the rulers of the Gentiles lord it over them, and their high officials exercise authority over them. Not so with you. Instead, whoever wants to become great among you must be your servant, and whoever wants to be first must be your slave—just as the Son of Man did not come to be served, but to serve, and to give his life as a ransom for many.

Jesus did not like hierarchical approaches to church leadership but instead espoused mutual submission and service. Neither the prophetic nor apostolic was designed to leverage authority over others. Apostles, in an order of listed gifts, are recorded first in 1 Corinthians 12:28, but anyone who teaches that apostles carry preeminence over other five-fold gifts does so erroneously. Indeed, no single one of the five ministry gifts is to consider itself the most important or to trump the influence and impact of the other giftings. Instead, they are all to serve the whole body of Christ and to depend upon each other to bring the body to maturity and completeness.

Those who inappropriately assume hierarchical power along with the title of prophet or apostle can wreak havoc. Scripture is clear about the need to test these people, and discernment remains a necessity. In reality, this is part of the reason there is reaction today regarding use of the terms, "apostles" and "prophets." Enough false prophets and false apostles have grasped for and assumed the titles that they are creating problems. People automatically put their guard up when hearing the label. If true prophetic and apostolic workers take on the title, they run the risk of not being taken seriously or thought prideful or deceitful. While various individuals today are clearly called by God and given to apostolic and prophetic functioning, granting them a formal title is unnecessary and unwise given these circumstances.

Theologian Wayne Grudem proposes, "If any in modern times want to take the title of 'apostle' to themselves, they immediately raise the suspicion that they may be motivated by inappropriate pride and desires for self-exaltation, along with excessive ambition and a desire for much more authority in the church than any one person should rightfully have."[67] Authentic prophetic and apostolic ministers cannot afford the risk of being branded as false or having the Spirit's work blocked by others' fear and mistrust. People need to feel safe for the full Spirit flow to work, and if that means not having a title, then so be it. Why should it matter to us? Function can occur perfectly well without a title being attached. Take Jesus: Though many people failed to recognize Him as the Messiah and the Son of God, He still was, and He accomplished every single thing He was called to do.

Function can occur perfectly well without a title being attached.

A great example of someone with the proper view of position and title is St. Martin of Tours who, in the 4th century, did a great apostolic work throughout Gaul, especially in the countryside with unreached pagan tribes. He did not want the title of "bishop" (an apostolic position), but the city of Tours, France was determined to have him in this capacity. They lured him to the town on the pretense that someone was ill and needed prayer, so he hurried in, not suspecting they intended to take him for the bishopric ceremony right then and there. Several historians relate that after he discovered this plot, he tried to hide among some hay stacks, but geese gave him away with their honking. This reluctance to have position and title easily serves as a model of humility and the right attitude toward leadership. Anything else is a grasping sham!

Today there is a surge of people calling themselves new apostles, something that arose in other times of Church history as well. In regards to this title, Vinson Synan also criticizes those who would call themselves apostles asserting, "Most people in church history who have claimed to be new apostles have been branded as heretics and excommunicated from the church."[68]

Besides the "apostles," many today also claim to be "prophets." They are making a name for themselves and providing numerous prophecies. Some throw the title around loosely and inappropriately, labeling as "prophetic" any kind of protest that is extreme, conspicuous, or stubborn. They claim the title of "prophet" for anyone whose ideas or behavior is questioned by authority, no matter how reasonably.

Genuine prophetic ministers are not "performers" giving "prophecy-on-demand."

Those who are authentically prophetic are typically very reluctant to call themselves prophets so as not to risk being wrongly placed into an incorrect camp. They just want to follow God and do not insist on thinking the Lord will give them a handy message every day to put up on a website or "words" at a specific time at a conference. Genuine prophetic ministers are not "performers" putting forth when someone snaps their fingers. "Prophecy-on-demand" is not possible for them. They wait until and if God speaks to them about something He has to say.

An interesting example of interaction between a false prophet and a genuine one occurs in Jeremiah 28. At that time, both of them were called "prophet," but one of them, Hananiah, had usurped the title. Jeremiah took issue with Hananiah's false prophecy which proclaimed the bondage of Babylon would be broken in two years. The hearers were excited at this positive word, and Jeremiah replied, "May the Lord do so" (v. 6). But then he said, "From early times the prophets who preceded you and me have prophesied war, disaster and plague against many countries and great kingdoms. But the prophet who prophesies peace will be recognized as one truly sent by the Lord only if his prediction comes true" (v. 8-9). Jeremiah didn't say more until the Lord told him to prophesy to Hananiah that instead of his wooden yoke being broken (what Hananiah had done as a sign), the people would be given an iron yoke. Jeremiah told Hananiah, "The Lord has not sent you, yet you have persuaded this nation to trust in lies. Therefore this is what the Lord says: 'I am about to remove you from the face of the earth. This very year you are going to die, because you have preached rebellion against the Lord'" (v. 1b-17).

Jeremiah's prophetic word from God came to pass, and Hananiah did indeed die that year. He had given a wrong word not from the Lord, and instead of being humble, he was arrogant and flaunting. He did not submit himself to a genuine prophet, Jeremiah, but pushed his own word that everybody wanted to hear (1 Cor. 14:32). God is not happy with those who play around with prophecy and say what is not true, what is sensational, or what people want to hear. This brings trouble to those who naively believe in that wrong word and also offers serious consequences for the false prophet.

The prophecy "business" that is occurring today needs to be carefully considered. Believers must be aware that not everyone who prophesies exciting words is worthy to be followed. Those calling themselves "prophets" are not necessarily functioning according to God's Word. There are real consequences to playing with false prophecy!

Chapter Twelve

Contemporary Problems: Now What?

*"We do not see our signs; there is no longer any prophet,
nor is there any among us who knows how long."*
Psalm 74:9

We now turn to some present concerns that have many implications for the prophetic and apostolic. In the first part of this chapter regarding problem areas, we (Joe and Carolyn) have chosen not to name any particular people or groups. Being inherently antithetical toward schism, division, or criticism, our intention is not to deride anyone in particular. Rather, for the sake of teaching discernment and being realistic as to potential error, we are including broad-spectrum information designed to increase understanding of this topic. You should be able to apply the testing keys for authentic apostolic and prophetic work to these situations.

Today's Disturbing Trends in "Apostles" And "Prophets"
At this time, various self-proclaimed "apostles" are arising and attracting literally millions of Christians across the country through assurances of signs, wonders, and personal experiences, and these are being supported by various fellow ministers aligning "under their spiritual covering." These "apostles" are basically functioning outside of the church, operating through social media, "how to" conferences, and technology (especially smart phones and Internet) to project their message while employing a variety of marketing

strategies to draw people by the droves. As a function of their own independent or personal ministries, they generally by-pass local churches in their efforts, even skipping over mega-churches. Throughout this process, they tend to function outside of Church accountability and oversight. Some do have a type of advisory board, often composed of like-minded friends and colleagues.

Referring to the "new apostles," Brad Christerson, professor of sociology at Biola University, states the following in an interview for *Christianity Today* by Bob Smietana, a Nashville-based religion writer:

> This group is unique in that they really think God has put these apostles on earth to basically transform the world. It's a sort of trickle-down Christianity, where these apostles are at the top of the mountain, exercising this power from the top down. That's how the kingdom of God comes in.[69]

Note this so-called "apostolic" work is not designed to go into the dark places around the world to establish the church. Growing the church is not really its final goal. Instead there is a mustering of an army of believers to come to conferences and to hear "words from the Lord," rather than primarily mobilizing and sending people to the harvest fields.

Smietana explains that their "real power lies in their innovative approach to selling faith. They've combined multi-level marketing, Pentecostal signs and wonders, and post-millennial optimism to connect directly with millions of spiritual customers. That allows them to reap millions in donations, conference fees, and book and DVD sales. And because these ... apostles claim to get direction straight from God, they operate with almost no oversight."[70]

The "new prophets and apostles" don't have to rely on donations or tithes from people in a church since they have a sort of pay-for-service model from high-profile conferences and media sales. Fans tend to choose one of these people so they can be "under their covering," saying things like "he is my apostle" or "she is my prophet." This seems to smack of Paul's negative description in 1 Corinthians 1:12b where such talk caused factions: "One of you says, 'I follow Paul'; another, 'I follow Apollos'; another, 'I follow Cephas'....." Remember that true apostolic and prophetic work brings unity.

These "new apostles and prophets" accumulate a following. Some have actually referred to themselves as "super-apostles" who have a broad influence with other apostles.[71] In one conference advertisement, there were not only prophets, apostles and bishops listed but also "covering apostles," "presiding apostles," "jurisdictional apostles," "archbishops," "prelates" (religious rulers), and even someone designated as the "super eminence apostle so and so."[72]

Said Christerson, "It's all sort of self-appointed. Leaders in the moment would say that people are recognized as apostles because of the influence that they have—not only over your own congregation but over other leaders. But there's definitely a good deal of self-appointing going on."[73]

God may take authentic apostolic workers to some out-of-the-way field where they fall off the map.

Such "self-appointing" carries the dangerous potential of circumventing the clear call of God as sensed through the Spirit's leading amidst a community of praying believers. Most Christians don't naturally desire to be selected for genuine apostolic or prophetic work since it usually generates real challenges and a personal price. Those genuinely called must pick up their cross daily, following where God leads, and that probably will not be all ease, popularity, and comfort. The Lord may take authentic apostolic workers to some out-of-the-way mission field where they fall off the map, or He may give them a difficult word to share where it is not at all appreciated.

The deep humility and brokenness required of genuine prophetic and apostolic workers means that a stage is not required to function. Notoriety may be exchanged for a life of unseen, gripping intercession. If people are not willing to make such exchanges as God directs, then they should be suspect. This means that grandiose working in signs and wonders as a show must also be considered, remembering that in the last days false Messiahs and false prophets will "perform great signs and wonders to deceive, if possible, even the elect" (Matt. 24:24).

Though we have seen that authentic apostolic ministry does

indeed work in signs and wonders, these are used to display the greatness of God in dark places so people will find their way to Christ's cross of hope, grace, and eternal salvation. The miracles demonstrate that the Lord is strong and mighty and deserves to be served as the one, true God. We are not here to pass off "power" amongst Christians for the purpose of having hyper personal experiences, as some of the "new apostles and prophets" appear to be doing.

Of end times false signs and wonders, 2 Thessalonians 2:9-10 states: "The coming of the lawless one will be in accordance with how Satan works. He will use all sorts of displays of power through signs and wonders that serve the lie, and all the ways that wickedness deceives those who are perishing." Church leaders must train their people to be open to the miraculous which is truly of God while discerning those "displays of power" which are not.

In further extremes, as a denominational state bishop/superintendent, I (Joe) have held conversations with concerned parishioners whose church was being "hijacked" by a leader giving consistently false prophecies, espousing incorrect doctrine of various kinds, and trying on their own to remove the church from its denominational roots. I have seen first-hand those proclaiming apostolic or prophetic authority who deny and shun God-ordained accountability, apparently believing themselves to be more spiritual, gifted, or experienced. In so doing, they show their true colors and disregard the spiritual callings of God's elect, as well as an important aspect of their own spiritual covering provided by God.

Additionally, I (Joe) have held letters incorrectly interpreting scriptural and other prophecies, demanding that I do certain things, like rebuke the one they have determined is the "beast" in Revelation. Prophetic deformations of all kinds can wreak havoc in a church if they are not handled and guided by leadership. One might think the whole thing is crazy. Certainly, those outside the Church do indeed. It is no wonder the Church struggles at times to reach today's society.

Unfortunately, a few who carry a genuine mantle of the prophetic or apostolic, as I (Joe) have experienced personally, choose to shun the church's spiritual oversight and accountability the more they gain prominence or reputation. Quick to lead, to tell others what they "feel and discern," or to proclaim what they personally promote, they forget to emulate the ministry character of Paul and the other apostles. They personally fall into the trap of needing a spiritual voice to fine-tune their steps, while alienating the very voices of protection and prayer support God designed for their lives at that time.

I (Carolyn) have been places in both the United States and overseas where self-appointed "apostles" have come in and said they are now "the apostle" over churches in that region. They demand control in decision-making and for ten percent of the tithes in the local church to be brought to them. Notably, they are "smooth" enough in their demands that churches actually come under them, thinking to receive power from God and to participate in ushering in the Kingdom of God "now" (the theology of these "new apostles" tends to be theologically post-millennial).

Biblically, the idea of having various apostles in charge of certain cities or territory does not seem to have precedent. Since the apostles were mobile, decisions in the early Christian churches appear to have been made mainly by local elders. The Assemblies of God position on this matter states this:

> None of the New Testament letters are addressed to an apostle, as would be expected if each city had its own ruling apostle. One of the few letters that includes church officers in the title, Philippians, is addressed to "overseers [*episkopos*] and deacons [*diakonos*]" (1:1)— not to a local or city apostle. There seems to be no concern to place recognized apostles in residence in the various churches or regions.[74]

Some of these false prophets even charge a fee if someone wants specific prayer and prophecies.

Besides the present day "new apostles" trying to exert broad influence over a city or area, the "new prophets" also exert influence through speaking and the large conference mode. Others have blogs followed by millions where they pass out regular (sometimes even daily) prophecies. In some of the conference settings these self-appointed "prophets" give multiple public prophecies which can become quite sensational. There is an expectation that prophecies will be given in certain settings, almost "on command." Some of these false prophets even charge a fee if someone wants specific prayer and prophecies.

This begins to sound like a psychic medium.

A good number of the prophetic words from the "new prophets" are grandiose generalizations and could apply to any number of situations. God knows us specifically and is wanting to guide us and our local churches rather than providing only broad, "feel good" words which are exciting and positive. For example, instead of pointing to Jesus, one "prophecy" claimed there would be seven millionaires in a particular church in the next year. Some of these contemporary "prophets" have been studied, and it was discovered that the majority of their specific prophecies did not come to pass, but they still continued giving "words," and people kept coming to hear them.

Applying Some of the Tests for Authentic Ministry
Although it is unnecessary here to apply each and every one of our tests to such situations, let us name a few concerns apostolically that appear to be present in some degree or another: love of money, assuming personal power, being self-appointed, looking for influence and popularity, grasping top-down authority over other people, marketing the "power" of the gospel, functioning with little or no oversight, and not carrying out actual apostolic work.

If we contrast such characteristics with a God-called apostle like Paul, we easily note that Paul did not ask for funds but still worked at his tentmaking so he could take care of himself and also give to others (Acts 20:33-35). We note his integrity, humility, and servanthood. Paul was willing to work with the local church leaders along with being accountable to other apostles in Jerusalem. He spent his years traveling miles to take the gospel to those who had not heard.

We pursue God and then He does what He chooses, and not on command either.

Neither Paul nor the other New Testament apostles considered concepts like "passing down" their power to other believers because they had special access to God and a great deal of influence over people. It is so foreign to their thinking that it is difficult to even conceive of it. Yes, they laid hands on people and looked to the Spirit to minister to hungry souls, but there was never an idea that they had something special to transmit because they had a great audience.

Their attitude became quite clear with Peter and Simon: "When Simon saw that the Spirit was given at the laying on of the apostles' hands, he offered them money and said, 'Give me also this ability so that everyone on whom I lay my hands may receive the Holy Spirit'" (Acts 8:18-19). Peter severely rebuked him and said that Simon should never think he could buy the gift of God with money. We are not meant to seek after power from somebody else. We pursue God, and we follow the Spirit; then He does what He chooses, and not on command either.

Prophetically, too, it is likewise impossible to provide prophecies on demand that people want to hear. Prophecies are not always meant to be "feel good" words. Hananiah learned this the hard way (Jer. 28). Prophecy was not designed to be a show in which people become amazed and pleased by what the "prophet" says.

Two extreme deformations can exist within contemporary "prophetic messages." One side looks at prophecy as entirely propitious in a sort of unrestrained mystical way, claiming to know what is happening in the heavenlies. Another extreme views prophecy as something that needs to be ominous, heavily confrontive, harsh, and merciless.

Some of the approaches for both the new "apostles and prophets" lend themselves to spectacular and dramatic ministry which brings a high level of excitement. Stated Christerson:

> Between the internet and the conferences, they have figured out ways to leverage that big, exhilarating, hyped-up experience you get in a stadium venue. That's where their networking comes into play. They can bring in four or five apostles, and then their followers flock to see them. People have these significant experiences that juice them up to contact the apostles over the internet. If they can go to a conference two or three times a year to get a new jolt, that becomes the new rhythm, as opposed to the weekly rhythm of church life.[75]

This is important to consider as we discern and sort proper apostolic functioning today. In some cases, the present "apostles and prophets" are by-passing the church, not facilitating partnership and involvement with local communities of worship. This process negates the entity God ordained to establish His Kingdom and eliminates the concept of the "priesthood of all believers." We have seen clearly throughout Acts that the apostles worked with the deacons and elders of the local churches in decision-making, prayer, and outreach. Together the churches chose and sent forth true apostles. God never intended for "apostles" and "prophets" to minister in a separate and unrelated stream without connection to the churches.

Likewise, the prophets were integrated within the community, even to the point of going into exile with the people. Any "prophets" today who do not join in as part of a worshipping church has no right to lob prophecies into it from the sidelines, especially negative ones.

> *The apostolic/prophetic was not designed as a separate stream unconnected to the Church.*

God established the church to be the entity through which He works, and He is not by-passing it now to build up a new authoritarian structure where the decrees of a few go unchallenged. The local church is meant to be mature and strong, governing itself congregationally for the advancement of God's Kingdom. This includes bringing into the fold both apostolic and prophetic workers, who may in turn be sent forth, but still under the auspices of caring, local congregations.

The decision about whether or not these "new apostles and prophets" fall into the false category should not be a massive dismissal of the entire group. There are varying degrees of problems, and some have good hearts and are simply misguided. Many of them see the deep need for authentic apostolic and prophetic streams to flow again within our churches. Desiring it so much, well-meaning people can often try to bring a change in the best way they know how. Before lobbing people into a false category, we should take the time to know them: their heart, their fruit, their prayer life, the way they love, how they accept accountability and correction, and more.

If some are discerned to be false apostles and prophets, we should stay away from them. Certainly, their ministry would stop flat if Christians saw the truth and stopped listening to them, attending their conferences, or looking up their prophecies every day. We should equip congregants to be better at discernment so they will not be deceived as they make individual choices.

He Who Has Ears to Hear

Christians today need to quit paying attention to what they should not heed. The well-known prophecy in 2 Timothy 4:3 bears an important reminder: "For the time will come when people will not put up with sound doctrine. Instead, to suit their own desires, they will gather around them a great number of teachers to say what their itching ears want to hear." This is happening right now. People are not only wanting to hear false doctrine that better fits our culture but also exciting "spiritual" details that are tangential to the truth. It can help them feel in the know and in control. In the meantime, people are slipping into hell and desperately need to hear something as well—and that is the pure, good news of Jesus Christ.

Christians must learn how to hear from God Himself. In the gospels, Jesus was often aware that people were not listening to Him. We are still impolite today, not listening to what the Spirit is saying or refusing to pay attention because we want to do things our own way.

Jesus was continually saying things like "He who has ears to hear, let him hear" (Matt. 13:9, 43 and 11:15; Mark 4:9,23 and 7:16). He really saw this to be a problem, or He would not have said it so often. Even in the last book of the Bible (Rev. 2:29), Jesus was still saying, "Whoever has ears, let them hear what the Spirit says to the churches." He wants us all to hear what the Spirit "is saying" to them in the present—not just what He said in the past.

God always has a response in mind to complete the communication circuit.

Not everyone knows how to listen carefully to God, either individually or corporately. Some are distracted, don't pay attention, and aren't sensitive to the quickening of the Spirit when God is speaking. The Lord cares about getting His message through, concerned with what He has to say as well as how it is received. He desires to be heard clearly and completely. The Church needs the prophetic to flow more freely. It should have many believers who are willing to pray, hear from the Lord, and prophesy. But this will mean little if people do not listen to the message.

God always has a response in mind to complete the

communication circuit. The prophetic servant senses what this response should be and is in pain if that rejoinder does not occur. It is distressing to deliver a carefully prepared message from the Lord and then have it either spurned or ignored. One feels the sorrow in the heart of the Father. This happens as well when the timing for a word is here and now, but no space is allowed for it to be delivered. Not listening to God when He is wanting to enter a conversation and speak is a serious disobedience. "He who has ears to hear, let him hear!" It is imperative today's Church leaders be sensitive to God's voice, willing to rest in His presence and be receptive to the gifts once again.

What Prophetic/Apostolic Work Looks Like In the Local Church
If people were to recognize God's call to apostolic and prophetic work, many in the Church would be involved in this flow of God's Spirit. We have seen in Scripture that God wants to "pour out" and use all kinds of Christians, not limited to just several "special" people. The leadership gifts were not provided for the fame and adulation of a favored few but rather for the equipping of all God's people for the work of the ministry.

When it comes to the prophetic in the church today, the gift of prophecy should be a normality within the church body, as should all the gifts of the Spirit. The prophetic should not only find release in church services as the Spirit desires, but also provide a natural flow of God-given prophetic insight, direction, and correction in staff, Board, and committee meetings. It should appear throughout the decision-making, planning, and administration of the church. Local prophetic workers will strengthen the intercession and prayer ministries and teach by modeling a deep prayer life. They will care about holiness and maintaining a clean and pure church. Main goals will be to build up the church, confirm God's direction, teach people to hear from the Lord, and model sensitivity to the Spirit. Strong prophetic leaders can help in their local churches but also write, speak, teach, and sow into other churches and leaders as the Lord directs.

Having many people who know how to move in the Spirit allows for prophetic checks and balances, providing safety and balance. The design is for confirmation and guidance from a variety of sources so the church may step out in assurance. Prophecy makes us stronger and bolder to carry out what God wants.

> *Prophecy makes us stronger and bolder to carry out what God wants.*

The work of the apostolic should likewise be powerfully evident in the Church today. While apostolic leaders are often found forging new territory outside the church or in foreign lands, we can frequently find some of these same traits and callings within local congregations. God wants to provide those who will stir up the local church to reach out into the community and touch different groups. These apostolically oriented church people are regularly dreaming creative ideas and are somehow able to make the connections and find the resources to bring them into reality.

Such people might appear never to be satisfied—always wanting new thrusts—so they can sometimes be a little frustrating to have around. They are not happy with the status quo and constantly seem to crave change. When one project is completed, they want to leave it with another person to run it and then move on to change something else.

The apostolic workers in the church include the entrepreneur, the person with creative imagination, the one who is always asking "what if?", the idea guy, the mover and the shaker, the risk-taker, the innovator, the networker, the gap filler, the resourcing individual, the denominational connector, promoters of missions, the one adept at contextualizing, the miracle worker, the mobilizer, the cross-culturally astute, the leader and participants of mission trips, and the one sensitive to special groups. If they are hearing from God, count them as a gift to the church instead of agitators.

Apostolicity is meant to flow around the world and within the local church. It moves into communities, regions, states, countries and continents. There are no boundaries, and we dare not wall it in. We require apostolic functioning to take us out of ourselves and heal our myopia. When we recognize and support the apostolic, the results are tremendous.

As a local church, it is clearly God's pleasure and plan that we participate in some significant thrusts into new territory. His strategies and ways are various and inclusive. For our own sakes, the local church needs to embrace this expanding and extending current sent from the heart of God.

What about those who are called full-time to apostolic work rather than the part-time support roles just enumerated? They are not among us too often, but that is why we need to have many people with apostolic bents working in the local church so we can make similar inroads into the dark places in our local communities.

When the full-time workers, like missionaries, are among us and off the field for a time, we need to allow them to sow apostolic fervor into the local churches. By sharing stories about needs and what God is doing, they train others in apostolic thinking, support, and praying. They can teach the church how to "see" the needs around them, sensitize them to people groups, and help them to become expansion-oriented. The church should also be instructed to understand the dynamic of their "sending" of apostolic workers to other places in the world. As the ones doing the sending, they must support the missionaries with funds, prayer, interest, and encouragement. A clear attachment needs to grow between the local church body and the ones they send. These same principles apply to planting satellite churches or sponsoring new church planters.

Another point of apostolic function today can emerge when leaders are put in positions which require apostolic thinking. Both of us have seen shifts in networks, states, churches, and colleges where the leader begins to perceive things apostolically. Consider Trinity Bible College and Graduate School in Ellendale, ND where shifting focus from mainly training pastors to also include many new apostolic thrusts around the globe has appealed to new students.

Likewise, fresh apostolic emphasis has occurred in new church plants which launched with an apostolic DNA. Some older, more established churches have also moved into spearheading new apostolic work.

Regional Leadership and Accepting God's Enablement

We (Joe and Carolyn) believe there are more potential apostolic leaders whom God desires to raise up with cutting-edge ministries into dark places, but this requires a certain way of thinking, strategizing, and reallocating funds. Denominational leadership can play a strong role in making these shifts and launching new missions and outreach, changing focus, modeling apostolic leadership, and providing momentum and energy. In some places where apostolic thinking has long been a sedentary affair, this leader shift can create some resistance. Nonetheless, it is worth the skirmish to move ahead with God's direction and see His new work accomplished.

Denominational leaders have clear apostolic responsibilities and functions.

The role of denominational leaders needs more focus in this discussion. Most denominations/fellowships organize with a bishop or superintendent serving churches in a specific state, region, or language/people group so their apostolic impact can be extensive. This distinctive role should definitely be considered from an apostolic perspective. The leader generally has clear apostolic responsibilities and functions. Think back to the functions of apostolicity as this list is given. They 1) are responsible for the health and well-being of the churches in their area; 2) see churches are planted in those places without a significant gospel witness; 3) help the local church maintain sound doctrine; 4) assist with necessary discipline matters and other problems; 5) provide various kinds of support for fledgling or failing churches; 6) raise offerings and encourage joint efforts of apostolicity; 7) find and provide resources of various kinds; 8) provide accountability services; 9) organize pastoral training both pre-service and in-service; 10) provide moral oversight and strengthening for ministers; 11) offer opportunities for various groups to gather for worship and encouragement; 12) participate in church and organizational governance; 13) provide missionary information, trips, and organized support; 14) network people and resources; 15) muster spiritual encouragement, prayer, insight, and health; 16) identify, train, and ordain new leaders, and 16) provide vision for God's preferred future.

After seeing this list and comparing it with the responsibilities of Christ's apostles, these bishops/superintendents obviously have apostolic work to accomplish. Most often such leaders are elected and come from pastorates, thus requiring the need of a conscious leader-shift to apostolic thinking. Certainly, those who vote for such positions need to pray and discern who is called to the apostolic ministry rather than voting only with pastoral qualities in mind. Specifically, those who accept such responsibilities must realize a new calling from God.

I (Carolyn) had a seer experience once when I prayed for someone who had an apostolic mantle placed on his shoulders by God, but it was hovering about two inches above his shoulders. I said, "Stand up! The mantle is there upon you, but you are feeling weak and inadequate for it. Stand up straight so the mantle falls upon your shoulders and you know that the Spirit has called you and is anointing you."

> *We find strength in recognizing the spiritual equipping that comes with our responsibilities.*

Both apostolic and prophetic ministers of all kinds will find strength in recognizing the calling, anointing, spiritual equipping, and God-given wisdom and authority that come with their responsibilities. Along with the spiritual roles of pastors, teachers, and evangelists, the seasoned mantles of those who humbly function in genuine prophetic and apostolic giftings are essential for a balanced maturity in the church. Those called by God clearly need to recognize their callings and responsibilities and then consciously accept the enablement God has for them.

According to Australian evangelist, Christine Caine, "Our world needs an anointed generation, not just a gifted generation."[76] The anointing and calling of the apostolic and prophetic gifts belong to God Himself and are given by empowerment of the Holy Spirit. People cannot anoint themselves any more than they can be self-appointed "apostles" or "prophets." The gift of genuine functioning in these areas comes only from the Lord.

Finding revelatory truth to carry out apostolic or prophetic functions is challenging, considering frequent excesses. Yet, to that end, denominational leaders must strive to discover and accept the will of God. They should determine to lead the Church faithfully in achieving God's purposes and demonstrating the full measure of His anointing. Caine also notes that within the AG, "... persons are not recognized by the title of apostle or prophet. However, many within the church exercise the ministry function."[77] To achieve the kind of strength obviously needed in the five-fold roles, it behooves leaders to accept their God-given mantles and function in union with the Spirit in accomplishing His full work today.

Ready to Encourage, Stop, and Teach

Church leaders today should not be either gullible to abuse or impervious to the Spirit of Christ. Paul writes in 2 Corinthians 4:4, "The god of this age has blinded the minds of unbelievers, so that they cannot see the light of the gospel of the glory of Christ, who is the image of God." While not blinded to the gospel as unbelievers, church leaders are sometimes skeptical, cynical, doubting, and suspicious of spiritual manifestations. Yet, no longer should they ignore carnal and abusive individuals and actions. What then should be done?

When leaders find themselves in a world of mêlée, trials, and complications with these topics, such matters necessitate a discerning pastor filled with the Holy Spirit who is prayerfully and humbly ready to address the situation without hesitation.

I (Joe) learned the importance of this amidst the ebb and flow of revival meetings when God's people were offering their various words, prayers, prophecies, challenges, discernments, and more. I found that the leader must pastor the work of God and address the issues of people surfacing in the church. Moments in the body of Christ that go without pastoral leadership may destroy hearts and hunger from genuine seekers. When not pastored, situations can let in confusion, displaced emotions, or skewed theologies from misguided individuals. As it's occurring, as unexpected as it might be, leaders must hear from God and pastor the moment. To delay until another time may be too late.

If there is a public prophecy, for example, and that prophecy is not accurate, a correction should probably be made immediately so the word does not confuse the body of believers. I (Carolyn) have stood up in public when an outside "prophet" visited a student meeting unannounced and began prophesying what I discerned was not at all correct. The spirit of the individual and hence the way the word was delivered both seemed off, so I stopped it and said I did not believe this word was correct for this time, and I would be happy to talk more with the individual after the meeting. They stomped out.

Those genuinely called to the prophetic or apostolic will seek out and treasure mentoring. The availability of sound, biblical teaching in these areas is practically nonexistent. Sometimes, in an effort to learn, individuals will pick up books which may not have the best advice. They can get involved in incorrect teaching just because they do not know where else to go.

The availability of sound, biblical teaching in the apostolic and prophetic is practically nonexistent.

Although copious training exists for the other four gifts in the five-fold ministry, this is not true for the prophetic especially. There are whole majors for teachers and pastors, even specialized classes for youth pastors and children's pastors. Courses exist for evangelists. Cross-cultural ministries majors train for missions, and there are classes and conferences for church planters. But few Christian schools have a class in the prophetic. Although the "schools of the prophets" were strong in the Old Testament, if young people feel such a call today, they really do not know what to do or where to turn. Where are those seasoned Pentecostal mentors with tested experience who have a sound scriptural base regarding the prophetic? How does one locate a prophetic internship? With few identified prophetic models and little solid instruction, is it any wonder that people make mistakes?

We definitely need to offer an instructional component in the churches if the God-ordained prophetic and apostolic streams are to be more widely released. Those called into these areas must have training, but the whole church should learn more too. Churches need to provide teaching opportunities in each of the five-fold gifts and help their people understand where they fit in their roles in the Body of Christ.

Everyone in the church should know and do the following regarding the apostolic and prophetic in particular: 1) "Eagerly desire gifts of the Spirit, especially prophecy" (1 Cor. 14:1). 2) Yearn to hear what God has to say in the Word and prophetically. 3) Gain the equipping necessary to do the work of the ministry. 4) Become gripped by the need for apostolic expansion. 5) Know what apostolicity and prophetic ministry looks like and gain appreciation and support for these. 5) Learn discernment so they can tell the difference between the true and false and not get hoodwinked.

If we are lacking in the prophetic and apostolic in our

churches today, it is not due to a disinterest by God but rather a lack of seeking on behalf of the church. We must stir up these gifts as we teach, encourage, and mentor the genuine, while simultaneously correcting or stopping the false.

Concluding Thoughts

A crisis exists in our contemporary understanding of both the prophetic and apostolic ministries. As a result, many Christians have been wary about these two functions.

Some denominations/fellowships have done an excellent job of carrying out Christ's great commission and sending out missionaries and others around the world to unreached people groups and into the dark and hidden corners where the truth of Jesus is still unknown. But the task is not yet accomplished. In some cases, people function apostolically without even being aware of their calling, anointing, and enablement. In other situations, the church has not clearly identified who is involved in apostolicity. Still others have not heard their call to apostolic work because they are unsure what it even entails. In the midst of all this, we desperately need more workers with a strong anointing upon them for apostolic functioning, and we must work toward developing a greater, conscious apostolic culture. This apostolic culture needs to penetrate not only denominations but districts/networks, Christian schools, and churches.

In many people's minds, the prophetic has been limited to the spiritual gift of prophecy, if even that. The broader, everyday functioning of the prophetic has not generally been fully released or understood. Many have not cultivated a listening ear, missing the very things God wants to communicate. Some genuine prophetic individuals have gotten discouraged, have been slapped down, or are unsure of how to proceed. They simply want to obey God and do what's right, but there is nowhere to learn and grow in safety. Few places exist for those in today's main-line churches, even those within classic Pentecostal circles, to find support, camaraderie, or further training without searching in varying charismatic or independent venues.

In the middle of weak and faltering understanding of both the apostolic and prophetic gifts, Satan has asserted false prophets and false apostles who cause people to be even more wary. Many are being deceived and blinded, running after self-identified "apostles" and "prophets" with self-aggrandizing, manipulative, or even heretical agendas (2 Cor. 11:1-15). Lack of discernment is rampant, and people are being hoodwinked.

Will leaders yearn for the fullness of God's work and Spirit-directed initiatives? Or will essential mission directives and the message of God's heart be set aside or locked in a closet? Will the contemporary Church remain satisfied with doing things its own way? Do leaders think they have a handle on it all with their own programs, their own message, and their own plans? Will they remain content to be in charge of the Church rather than letting God do it? If the Holy Spirit were to be removed from the earth today, when would He be missed?

Surely it is time to let the Lord have His church back. Since Jesus treasured the apostolic and prophetic enough to make them two-fifths of His five treasured gifts to the Church, we should allow these functions to flow again in the complete fullness He planned and desired.

Now is the time to teach on these ministries so people will understand. Blossoming prophetic and apostolic workers need to be encouraged, mentored, and taught the biblical foundations for these two functions. Even those not called to these ministries should be able to recognize their proper functioning as well as those masquerading. Leaders need to handle the bizarre, while simultaneously encouraging and embracing the genuine to the complete extent God intended.

You have the keys. Now what will you do?

Endnotes

1. Rick Dubose, General Presbytery Meeting, The State of the Church, July 31, 2018, Houston, TX.
2. Martin, E. Scott, Editorial, Chi Alpha Connection, Spring 2017, Volume 9, Issue 4.
3. Christian Population Growth, Wikipedia, accessed November 29, 2018. https://en.wikipedia.org/wiki/Christian_population_growth
4. Joseph S. Girdler, *The Superintendent Leader-shift from Pastoral to Apostolic Function: Awareness and Training in Leadership Development for District Superintendents in the Assemblies of God USA*, Assemblies of God Theological Seminary at Evangel University, D.Min., May, 2018.
5. Carolyn Tennant. *Catch the Wind of the Spirit: How the Five Ministry Gifts Can Transform Your Church (Springfield, MO: Vital Resources), 2016.*
6. Vinson Synan, "Apostolic Practice." Regent University, unpublished paper, n.d., 1. https://www.regent.edu/acad/schdiv/docs/faculty/synan/Apostolic_practice_Synan.pdf
7. Leonard Ravenhill, *Why Revival Tarries* (Minneapolis, MN: Bethany House, 1987), 151.
8. A. T. Robertson, "Act 13:1," in *Word Pictures in the New Testament* (Nashville: Broadman, 1933), Logos Bible Software.
9. E.M. Bounds, *The Complete Words of E.M. Bounds* (Radford, VA: Wilder Publications, 2008), 7.
10. Alan R. Johnson, *Apostolic Function in 21st Century Missions* (Pasadena, CA: William Carey Library, 2009), 73.
11. Amos D. Millard, *Learning from the Apostles* (Springfield, MO: Gospel Publishing House, 1971), 9.
12. David Cannistraci. *Apostles and the Emerging Apostolic Movement: A Biblical Look at Apostleship and How God Is Using It to Bless His Church Today.* (Ventura, CA: Renew Books, 1998), 79.
13. Daniel Henderson, *Old Paths New Power* (Chicago: Moody Publishers, 2016), 36.
14. Leonard Ravenhill, *Revival God's Way: A Message for the Church* (Minneapolis: Bethany House Publishers, 2006), 135.
15. Jim Cymbala, *Storm* (Grand Rapids, MI: Zondervan, 2014), 138-139.

16. Ruthie Edgerly Oberg . "This Week in AG History—April 11, 1942. AG News Update, April 11, 2019. accessed April 12, 2019. https://news.ag.org/en/Features/This-Week-in-AG-History-April-11-1942
17. Roland Allen and David M. Paton (ed.). *The Ministry of the Spirit: Selected Writings of Roland Allen*. Cambridge: The Lutterworth Press, 50.
18. John Eckhardt, *50 Truths Concerning Apostolic Ministry*, (Chicago: Crusader Ministries, 1994), 46.
19. Jeff Oliver, *Pentecost to the Present: Early Prophetic and Spiritual Gifts Movements – Book One* (Newberry, FL: Bridge-Logos, 2017), 9.
20. Craig S. Keener, *Miracles: The Credibility of the New Testament Accounts. Vols.1 & 2.* (Grand Rapids: Baker Academic, 2011).
21. John J Burkhard. *Apostolicity Then and Now: An Ecumenical Church in a Postmodern World.* (Collegeville, MN: Liturgical Press, 2004), 31.
22. Cannistraci, 170.
23. Tennant, 24-28.
24. James D.G. Dunn, *The Theology of Paul the Apostle* (Grand Rapids: Eerdmans, 1998), 574.
25. N. T. Wright, *Surprised by Scripture: Engaging Contemporary Issues* (San Francisco: HarperOne, 2014), 150.
26. Jeff Leake, *God in Motion: Making Sense of the Loose Ends in Life* (Springfield, MO: Influence Resources, 2013), 49.
27. Charles Wesley, "Jesus, Lord, We Look to Thee." Hymn, Public Domain., 1749. Hymnary.org, accessed November 8, 2018. https://hymnary.org/text/jesus_lord_we_look_to_thee
28. Jim Van Yperen, *Making Peace: A Guide to Overcoming Church Conflict* (Chicago: Moody, 2002), 186.
29. Ibid., 196.
30. Rick Rusaw and Eric Swanson, *The Externally Focused Church* (Loveland, CO: Group, 2004), 100.
31. Clarence St. John, comment and discussion at meeting of the USA Assemblies of God Superintendent's Cohort, Roselle, IL, August 24, 2014.
32. Van Yperen, 100.
33. Neil Cole. "How Many Churches Did the Apostle Paul Start?" accessed August 5, 2018. http://www.churchplanting.com/

how-many-churches-did-the-apostle-paul-start/#.W2dzVfZFyUk
34. *InterVarsity Press New Testament Commentaries*, "Acts 10," accessed August 11, 2018. https://www.biblegateway.com/resources/commentaries/IVP-NT/Acts/Peters-Vision
35. T.W. Manson. "Jesus and the Non-Jews." The Ethel M. Wood Lecture, University of London, March 3, 1954. accessed August 6, 2018. https://www.biblicalstudies.org.uk/pdf/jesus_manson.pdf
36. Ibid., 18.
37. Numerous sources encourage women in ministry. See: Gilbert Bilezikian, Beyond Sex Roles (Grand Rapids, MI: Baker Book House, 1985), 125-128. See also: Stanley Grenz, *Women in the Church* (Downers Grove, IL: InterVarsity Press, 1995), 38-55. See also: R. A. Tucker and W. Liefield, *Daughters of the Church* (Grand Rapids, MI: Zondervan, 1987), 73, 364. See also: Eldon Epp, *Junia: The First Woman Apostle* (Minneapolis, MN: Augsburg Fortress), 2005.
38. David Cartledge. *The Apostolic Revolution.* (Chester Hill, NSW, Australia: Paraclete Institute, 2000), 322
39. Joseph S. Girdler, 100.
40. Doug Clay, comment and discussion at the USA Assemblies of God Superintendent's Cohort, Roselle, IL, August 22, 2014.
41. Eckhard J. Schnabel, *Paul the Missionary: Realities, Strategies and Methods* (Downers Grove, IL: InterVarsity Press, 2008), 225.
42. Elizabeth Barrett Browning. "86. From 'Aurora Leigh,'" *The Oxford Book of English Mystical Verse*. Nicholson and Lee eds., (Oxford: The Clarendon Press, 1917), 644.
43. n.a. "Assemblies of God Position Paper on the Apostles and Prophets," 2001. Assemblies of God USA website, Beliefs, accessed November 19, 2018. https://ag.org/Beliefs/Topics-Index/Apostles-and-Prophet.
Note the following biblical references on this topic: 1 Cor. 14:29-32, 37 and 11:5-6; Romans 12:6.; 1 Thess. 5:20; Ephesians 2:20, 3:5, and 4:11; 1 Tim. 4:14
44. Ibid.
45. *Oxford Living Dictionaries*, English, "Testify," accessed September 6, 2018. https://en.oxforddictionaries.com/definition/testify
46. Elmer L. Towns, *God Encounters: To Touch God and Be Touched by Him* (Ventura, CA: Regal, 2000), 65.
47. Melvin Hodges. *Pentecostal Evangel*. Sept. 29, 1957. p.4.

48. Walter Bruggeman. *The Prophetic Imagination* 40th Anniversary Ed. (Minneapolis: Fortress Press, 2018), 45.
49. Charles Wesley. "And Can It Be that I Should Gain." Hymn. Public Domain, 1738. Hymnary.org, accessed November 7, 2018. https://hymnary.org/text/and_can_it_be_that_i_should_gain
50. J. B. Gabel and C. B. Wheeler, The Bible as Literature, 2nd. ed. (New York/Oxford University Press, 1990), 37 and 293
51. Jess A. Benner. "Poetry in the Hebrew Bible." accessed June 30, 2018. http://www.ancient-hebrew.org/language_poetry.html
52. Norman K. Gottwatt, "Hebrew Poetry," in *Interpreter's Dictionary of the Bible,* ed. George Buttrick (Nashville: Abingdon, 1962) 3:829-38.
53. Eugene E. Carpenter. Wayne McCown ed. *Asbury Bible Commentary,* "Prophetic Literature," Grand Rapids, MI: Zondervan, 1992, accessed June 28, 2018. https://www.biblegateway.com/resources/asbury-bible-commentary/Prophetic-Literature.
54. David Cloud, *Understanding Bible Prophecy.* Port Huron, MI: Way of Life Literature, 2018, accessed June 28, 2018. https://www.wayoflife.org/reports/figurative_language_in_bible_prophecy.php
55. Rudyard Kipling. "The Elephant's Child" in *Just So Stories for Little Children*. Reprint of Doubleday & Co. 1912 edition. (Old Saybrook, Connecticut: Konecky and Konecky, 2001).
56. Charles Wesley. "Come, Holy Ghost, Our Hearts Inspire." Hymn. Public domain, 1740. Hymnary.org., accessed November 18, 2018. https://hymnary.org/text/come_holy_ghost_our_hearts_inspire_let_u
57. Joshua Scroggins, *Awakening the Christian Imagination: Imagination and Creativity in Spiritual Formation.* Amazon Digital Service, 2018), Kindle, 29.
58. Abraham Joshua Heschel. *The Prophets* (New York: Perennial, 2001), 554.
59. Andy Stanley. *Making Vision Stick: Part 2—State It Simply*. Podcast. accessed June 30, 2018. https://www.leadercast.com/programs/making-vision-stick-part-2-state-it-simply
60. Walter Martin. *The Kingdom of the Cults: An Analysis of the Cult Systems in the Present Christian Era*. Rev. updated ed. (Minneapolis: Bethany Fellowship Books, 2003), 555.

61. Robert K. Greenleaf. *The Servant as Leader*. The Greenleaf Center for Servant Leadership, 2008. http://www.benning.army.mil/infantry/199th/OCS/content/pdf/
62. Charles Spurgeon. *Christian Quotes. 22 Quotes about discernment*. accessed November 19, 2018. https://www.christianquotes.info/quotes-by-topic/quotes-about-discernment/#axzz5XHbyZqKU
63. Paul Simon. "The Sounds of Silence" in *Wednesday Morning, 3 A.M.* sung by Paul Simon and Art Garfunkle, (New York: Columbia Records.1964).
64. A.W. Tozer. *Keys to Deeper Life*. 1st ed. 1959. Norman, OK: Pioneer Library Digital Edition, 2014. Section "Gifts of the Spirit: Are They for Us Today?" Location 272 Kindle
65. Christopher Hitchens in Foreword to *Aldous Huxley's Brave New World*. Reprint Edition (New York: Harper Perennial Modern Classics, 2005), xv.
66. Synan. "Apostolic Practice."
67. Wayne Grudem, *Systematic Theology, An Introduction to Biblical Doctrine* (Grand Rapids, MI: Zondervan, 1994), 911.
68. Vinson Synan, "Who are the Modern Apostles?" *Ministries Today* (March/April 1992): 42.
69. Bob Smietana, "The 'Prophets' and 'Apostles' Leading the Quiet Revolution in American Religion," *Christianity Today*. Aug. 3, 2017, Interview, accessed December 2, 2018. https://www.christianitytoday.com/ct/2017/august-web-only/bethel-church-international-house-prayer-prophets-apostles.html
70. Ibid.
71. Ibid.
72. Hyatt, Eddie. "When Revival Goes Wrong." Charisma News. Jan. 25, 2019. https://www.charismanews.com/opinion/74936-when-revival-goes-wrong
73. Smietana.
74. n.a. "Assemblies of God Position Paper on the Apostles and Prophets."
75. Smietana.
76. Christine Caine, "Your Destiny Now," aired December 3, 2016, on Trinity Broadcast Network.
77. Ibid.

About the Authors

Joseph S. Girdler, D.Min

Superintendent, Kentucky
Assemblies of God (USA)

Joseph S. Girdler, D.Min., is married to Dr. Renee V. Girdler, an American Board-Certified family physician. They have two children, Dr. Steven J. Girdler (and Julia), NYC, and Rachel R. Girdler, MSW, a missionary associate in Ecuador. Joe and Renee live in a suburb of Louisville, Kentucky. Being raised Southern Baptist and Missionary Baptist, then attending a primarily United Methodist seminary for his master's degree (following two undergraduate degrees from the University of Kentucky), Joe was ordained in 1994 with the Assemblies of God. He attained his D.Min. at Assemblies of God Theological Seminary of Evangel University and has ministered across the United States and internationally in dozens of nations. Joe is a member of the Assemblies of God General Presbytery, Commission on Chaplains, Commission on Ethnicity, and more, and served as Lead Pastor of King's Way Assembly of God in Versailles/Lexington, Kentucky (1988-2004). As a denominational Missions Director (1997-2005), his church was recognized from thousands of AGUSA congregations for achieving Top 100 status in World Missions giving, while Renee was honored as the first woman in Assemblies of God history to serve the denomination's World Missions Board. Pastor Joe has served from 2004 – present as the Kentucky Assemblies of God district superintendent.

Carolyn Tennant, Ph.D

Professor emerita, North Central University, Minneapolis, MN.

Adjunct professor, AOG Theological Seminary of Evangel University, Springfield, MO.

Carolyn Tennant, Ph.D., is professor emerita at North Central University, Minneapolis, MN, and an adjunct professor teaching regularly in the doctor of ministry program at the Assemblies of God Theological Seminary of Evangel University, Springfield, MO. She served for nearly thirty years at North Central University as a professor, vice president of academic affairs, and vice president of student life. Carolyn is ordained in the Assemblies of God, has a broad preaching ministry internationally and in the United States, and is a member of the AG Commission on Doctrinal Purity. Her last book, *Catch the Wind of the Spirit: How the Five Ministry Gifts Can Transform Your Church*, was a precursor to this book that focuses on the apostolic and prophetic ministries. She currently resides in Minneapolis with her husband, Ray.

Also by the Authors

Joseph S. Girdler

Setting the Atmosphere for the Day of Worship

Meadow Stream Publishing (March 5, 2019)
ISBN-13: 978-1733795203

Joseph S. Girdler

**Redemptive Missiology in Pneumatic Context:
Practical Missions Led by the Holy Spirit**

Meadow Stream Publishing (April 3, 2019)
ISBN-13: 978-1733795227

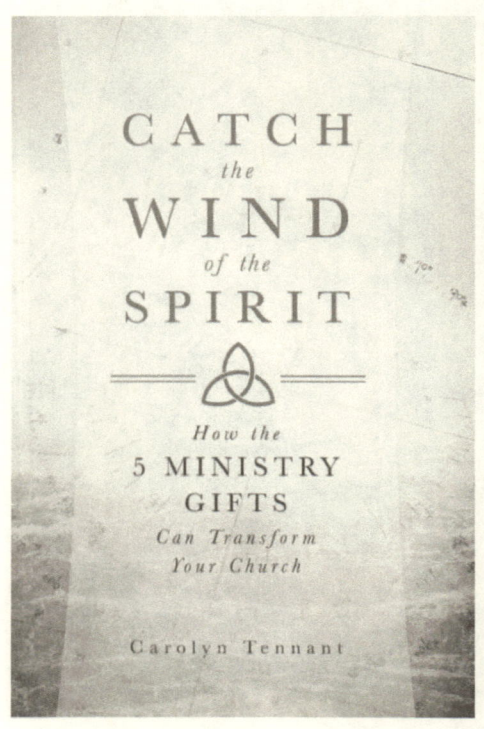

Carolyn Tennant

Catch the Wind of the Spirit: How the 5 Ministry Gifts Can Transform Your Church

Vital Resources (March 1, 2016)
ISBN-13: 978-1680660388

Carolyn Tennant

Front Line: A Daily Devotional Guide for Christian Leaders

North Central University Press (2004)
ISBN-13: 978-0976246107

www.ingramcontent.com/pod-product-compliance
Lightning Source LLC
Chambersburg PA
CBHW020407080526
44584CB00014B/1214